Barry Cunliffe

CRADLE OF ENGLAND

an introduction through archaeology to
the early history of England and a brief
guide to selected sites in the South

British Broadcasting Corporation

Acknowledgement is due to the following for their permission to
reproduce illustrations in this book:
Aerofilms, 20, 25 (top), 27; Ashmolean Museum, 19 (top); Avoncroft
Museum, 22 (top); Bignor Roman Villa, 32 (top); Brighton Art Gallery
and Museums, 21 (top); British Museum, 21 (bottom), 24; City of
St Albans, Verulamium Museum, 28; Mansell Collection, 25 (bottom),
32 (middle and bottom); J. K. St Joseph, 17, 18, 19 (bottom), 22
(bottom), 23, 26, 30, 31 (top).
We are grateful for permission to reproduce diagrams from:
Ancient Europe by Stuart Piggott, Edinburgh University Press,
(page 45); *Antiquity* (pages 66 and 67); Royal Commission on
Historical Monuments (England), Crown Copyright, (pages 42, 46
and 51).

Published by the
British Broadcasting Corporation
35 Marylebone High Street
London W1M 4AA
ISBN 0 563 12197 1
First published 1972
© Barry Cunliffe 1972
Printed in Scotland by
James Paton Limited,
18/20 Gordon Street,
Paisley PA1 1BX

Introduction

In less than 5000 years, from the time when the first farmers arrived on British shores until the Emperor Honorius formally gave up responsibility for the country in AD 410, the face of Britain and the lives of its people changed out of all recognition. At the beginning of this period the countryside was covered with forest and scrub and the people lived by hunting and gathering; towards the end the land was being farmed and managed in an orderly fashion by men who would have thought of themselves as members of a vast civilised empire and many of whom lived a life of culture and sophistication. The change was not sudden. It came about as the result of a series of advances, some slight, some dramatic, caused partly by the absorption of new ideas from outside and partly from the dynamic forces at work within society itself.

It is only within the last hundred years that we have begun to understand our past development. Two hundred years ago historians looking at the pre-Roman period could talk only of Ancient Britons. Then, early in the nineteenth century, it was suggested that Man had passed through three ages: of Stone, Bronze and Iron. This was a useful idea, a modified form of which is still sometimes adopted today in general descriptions. But simple schemes of this kind can only provide a generalised picture against which to describe Man's development; they cannot explain the processes or forces at work. For these necessary explanations, it was customary until recently to rely heavily upon the old ideals of Victorian imperialism. Thus a major change in a primitive community was usually believed to be the result of invasion because savages were not thought capable of progress. Nowadays, however, archaeologists are coming more and more to realise that ancient societies had within themselves the power to make dramatic leaps forward. Our growing awareness of Man's immense skill and inventiveness is perhaps one of the most exciting recent developments in archaeology: gone for good are old-fashioned notions of primitive savages.

The study of archaeology is now developing very rapidly: new techniques are being used to analyse the material remains left by ancient Man, excavations of increasing complexity are being carried out, while detailed field surveys combined with aerial photography are beginning to show just how densely occupied the British landscape really was. So much new evidence is now becoming available that archaeologists can at last begin to turn away from studies based only on the objects that have chanced to survive and can begin to look at the men themselves and at their social development.

The south of England is one of the richest areas in Europe for visible and varied archaeological remains. Admittedly there are some areas that may produce better examples or denser distributions of certain types of site but there is no region where so much can be seen so closely packed together. The south of England with its splendid monuments and magnificent museum collections is a vast open laboratory for anyone who wishes to begin to understand the past.

The theme of the following story is Man's development as a social animal. It is described against the backcloth of the archaeological remains of southern Britain and covers the period from about 4000 BC until AD 410.

1. The Rise of a Theocracy

Until about 6000 years ago Man in Britain was a hunter and collector living on berries, roots and fruit and those animals, including birds and fish, which he could trap, shoot or otherwise collect. Life was necessarily nomadic and because the food-producing potential of a territory was always limited, the size of communities remained restricted. There must have been times during the year when food was scarce but on the whole the forests, scrublands, rivers and sea-shores would have provided quite adequate nourishment for an efficient hunting group gradually working its way round its territory, knowing exactly where and when to search for every kind of food. Hunting the large wild cow, the elk and the red deer would have been the work of the men but women and children could have played a part in such pursuits as collecting berries and shellfish and perhaps fishing with basket traps and hooks and spears. Technology was well adapted to life-style – the weapons tipped with blades of flint were easy to make and light to carry while the by-products of hunting such as leather, sinew and bone were useful for making clothes, containers and tools. A food-gathering economy, however, imposed certain limits on social development, the most important being that mobility prevented the emergence of large stable communities capable of supporting specialists, and without specialists there could be little experiment and little pooling of ideas and abstract thoughts.

About 4000 BC new people, bringing with them a knowledge of food production, began arriving in Britain in boats laden with cultivated seed corn and domesticated cattle, sheep and probably goats. The story of their early, and no doubt precarious, attempts to gain a hold on the British countryside cannot yet be written but their eventual success is demonstrated by the gradual emergence of well-established farming communities. Animal husbandry and the strict processes involved in cultivation meant that communities became gradually more settled. In the archaeological record these neolithic peoples can be recognised in terms of their rectangular houses and their pottery, both implying a new and more stable way of life.

The basic tool kit showed significant changes, too: the multiple bladed spears and arrows disappeared while chipped stone axes, frequently polished to a fine smooth finish, make an appearance, reflecting the process of forest clearance which now began in earnest. Forest clearance is perhaps too grand a phrase; in practice small plots would have been carved out of scrubland by a process of slash-and-burn, leaving any charred stumps to rot, while the collection of leaves, principally elm, as fodder for cattle would have gradually halted natural re-generation and led to clearings appearing naturally in the forest cover, probably to have been enlarged and made use of by Man. By these destructive methods the land began to be cleared but we must not imagine a single relentless process. Land exhausted of its goodness would have been abandoned for many years before being cultivated again and there were vast tracts of Britain that were not deforested until very recently. Nevertheless between about 4000 and 2000 BC the face of southern Britain changed dramatically and by the end of the period much of the chalk and limestone upland would have been given over to regular mixed farming of an organised and efficient kind.

The increasing stability of life and the production of a small surplus of food released new creative pressures in society. Non-food-producing specialists, like the flint miners who dug shafts into the chalk to extract good flint for making axes, could now be supported on a full-time and part-time basis. There soon developed a complex trading network which allowed stone axes, made in Ireland, Wales, Cornwall and the Lake District, to be distributed over the whole country. But the most dramatic evidence of the new social cohesion was the appearance of what can only be called monumental architecture – 'causewayed camps', burial mounds, linear earthworks known as cursus monuments and the great ritual centres now called henges – each involving the expenditure of an immense amount of energy and calling for social organisation on a highly advanced level.

A brief description of a selection of these monuments is offered in the descriptive section below and the details need not detain us, but before we can begin to guess at the meaning of these staggering structures some indication must be given of their size. Of the four largest henge monuments in southern England, Avebury, Durrington Walls, Marden and Mount Pleasant, Durrington Walls offers the most dramatic evidence largely as the result of a recent excavation. Here some 30 acres were enclosed by a massive bank and ditch, the latter being originally 50 ft wide and 19 ft deep and requiring nearly a million man-hours to dig. Inside, the excavators found two timber buildings: the larger, measuring 127 ft in diameter, was built of six consecutive rows of timbers with some of the individual uprights as much as $3\frac{1}{2}$ ft across. On a conservative estimate it must have taken nine acres of an oak forest to provide the timber for this building alone. Silbury Hill, which belongs to the same period, is an even more impressive feat of engineering. More than 12 million cu. ft of chalk were quarried out of an encircling ditch and piled up to form a truncated cone 130 ft high, the base of which covers about $5\frac{1}{4}$ acres, making it the largest man-made mound in Europe. These figures are impressive even today to people accustomed to massive earth-shifting machines, but when it is remembered that the only tools then available were antler picks and wedges, baskets, and shovels made of shoulder-blades, the scale of the neolithic achievement can be more readily appreciated.

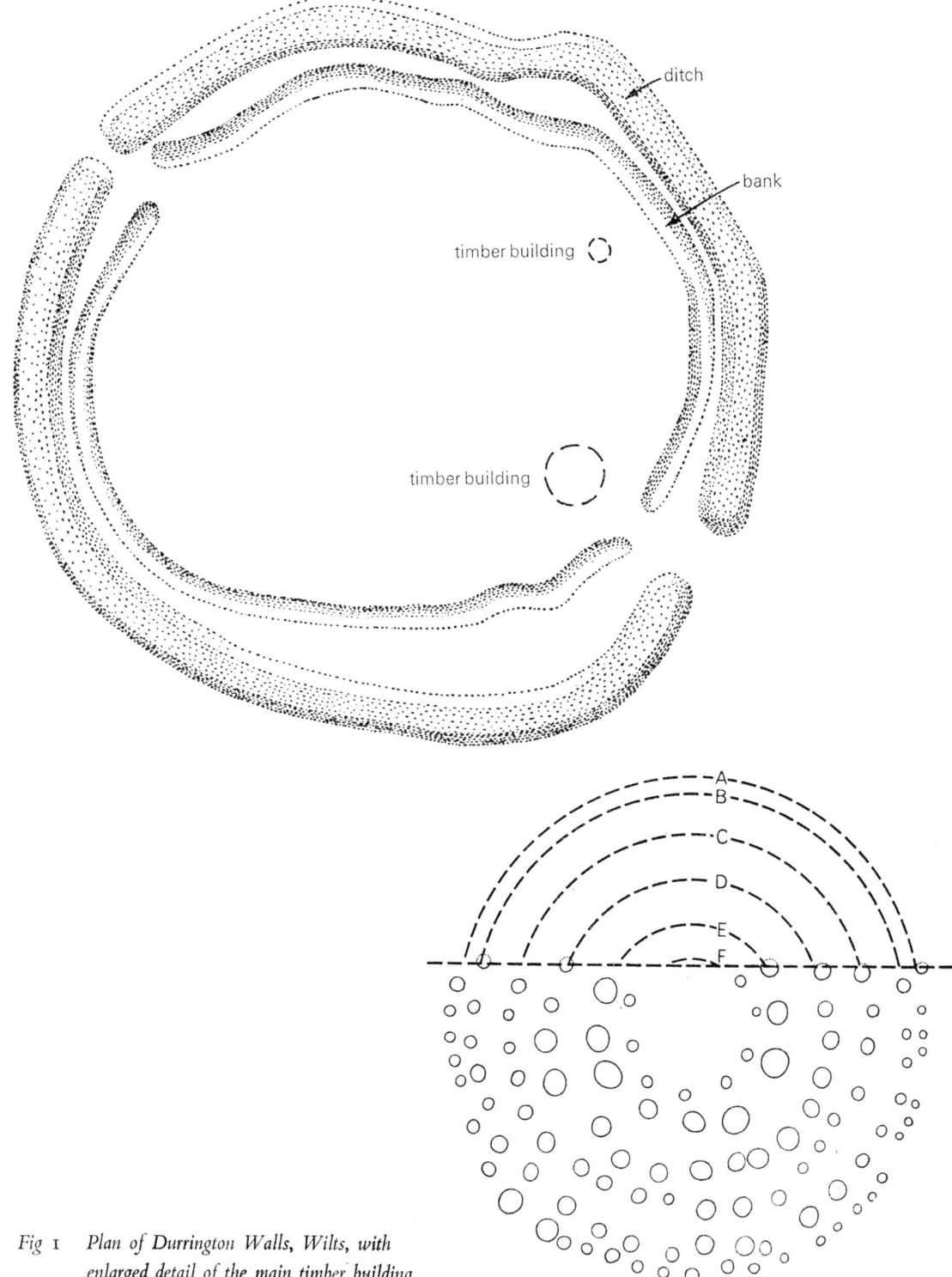

ditch

bank

timber building

timber building

A
B
C
D
E
F

Fig 1   *Plan of Durrington Walls, Wilts, with enlarged detail of the main timber building*

We are unlikely ever to understand fully the meaning of these great ritual monuments but it is inconceivable that they could have been built without some deep religious motivation. Silbury is unique and will always remain a mystery but the henges, with their enclosing ditches and vast timber buildings, might well have been ritual centres for tribal gatherings not unlike those in use by the Indians in parts of America in the last century. At the very least they imply a communal effort on an immense scale.

Most of the henges were built before 2000 B C and many of them continued in use for at least 500 years. One of the characteristics of their later use was the occasional erection of standing stones within the enclosures. Avebury, and Stonehenge in its later stages, are the best-known examples of such an arrange-ment but many other stone circles, elipses and alignments, without enclosing earthworks, are to be found in north and west Britain. For many years people have tried to interpret these structures, particularly Stonehenge, in astronomical terms, some suggesting that the settings of stones enabled complex predictions to be made, others suggesting that it was a computer. Many of the earlier theories were unfounded on fact but recently Professor Alexander Thom has carried out a series of very detailed measurements of stone circles in various parts of Britain and western France and has come to a number of dramatic conclusions. He has shown, for example, that the builders of these megalithic monuments were capable of abstract mathematical thought and accurate measurement and that many of the circles were erected in such a way as precisely to mark significant positions in the lunar cycle. Such skill implies, beyond reasonable doubt, that a few people could engage in complex experiment and observation and could record the results of these experiments, subsequently using the information to construct stone monuments of considerable sophistication. There must have been people present at this time who were far more intellectually able than most of us today.

It must be said that the full significance of Thom's theories have not yet been worked out by archaeologists but there is no real conflict between our know-ledge of the people seen through conventional archaeological evidence and the picture which the mathematical approach will have us believe of them. Neolithic society had, after a mere 2000 years of development in Britain, reached a stage in which vast resources of manpower could be brought together under inspired leadership to create great communal monuments like the henges. Clearly, there must have been men of very considerable organising ability able to utilise the energy which the surplus of food released. In such an atmosphere it is hardly surprising that the people who were, after all, farmers should have begun to wonder at the movements of the moon, sun and stars. They would surely have realised that these movements were related to the seasons, and the seasons to the growth and well-being of their crops and herds. Casual observation would have been followed by closer observation and eventually by the erection of the stone circles and alignments. Given surplus food, time and, above all, an intellectual curiosity, a people could reach great heights.

From what has already been said it is evident that society was well organised but of the actual method of cohesion and control we know very little though there are hints. The hill-top enclosures known as causewayed camps, like Windmill Hill near Avebury, are now generally considered to be places of tribal assembly where the community would meet in a group to worship the gods and to carry out the business of communal living – like buying and selling, the re-distribution of land and stock, and feasting. Meetings of this kind have always played an essential part in rural life and there is plenty of evidence for them later among the pre-Roman Celts and in the Roman world. Indeed, the medieval fair is a continuation of exactly the same tradition. The very existence of these centres implies a degree of social awareness, perhaps even a feeling of unity, going back to 3000 BC, many centuries before the building of the great henges, but it does not tell us where the power lay – that is, whether the driving force came from society as a whole or whether it was in the hands of elected or dynastic leaders.

We can, however, by studying the burial rites of the period, be tolerably certain that some kind of social hierarchy existed. The normal ritual involved the collective burial of a number of individuals whose bodies were accumulated in timber mortuary enclosures or stone-built collective tombs (like the West Kennet long barrow) until such time as it was decided to complete the burial by sealing the tomb or heaping a long mound of earth over the remains. Some writers have claimed to see sufficient similarities between the skeletal remains in one tomb to suggest that those buried were related to each other, the implication being that the tombs served as family vaults. At any event the careful and elaborate burial of certain individuals would suggest that they belonged to a socially distinct class. Perhaps they were the organisers and experimenters – the theocrats of neolithic society – who, spurred on by a deep belief in the gods, led the people to such incredible heights of achievement.

Southern Britain can boast some of the finest and most varied neolithic monuments in the country. A few of the more accessible have been selected for a brief description here.

Windmill Hill, *near Avebury, Wiltshire* (grid ref. SU 087714)
Reached by turning off the A361 at Avebury Trusloe about midway between Devizes and Swindon.

Windmill Hill supports a causewayed camp dating to the third millennium BC, represented by three broadly concentric lines of ditches, each of which is inter-

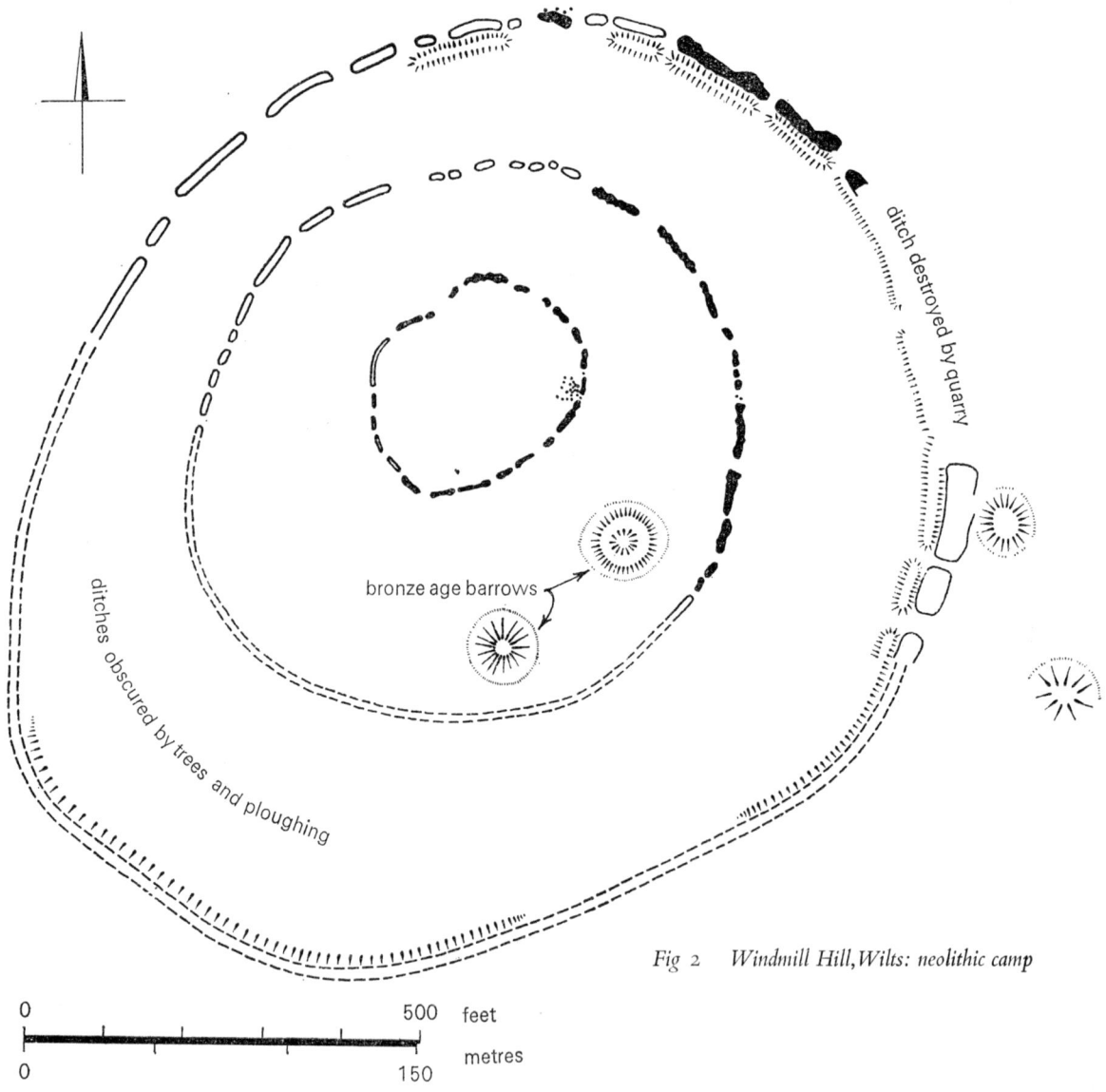

ditch destroyed by quarry

ditches obscured by trees and ploughing

bronze age barrows

Fig 2   Windmill Hill, Wilts: neolithic camp

| 0 | | | | 500 | feet |

| 0 | | | 150 | metres |

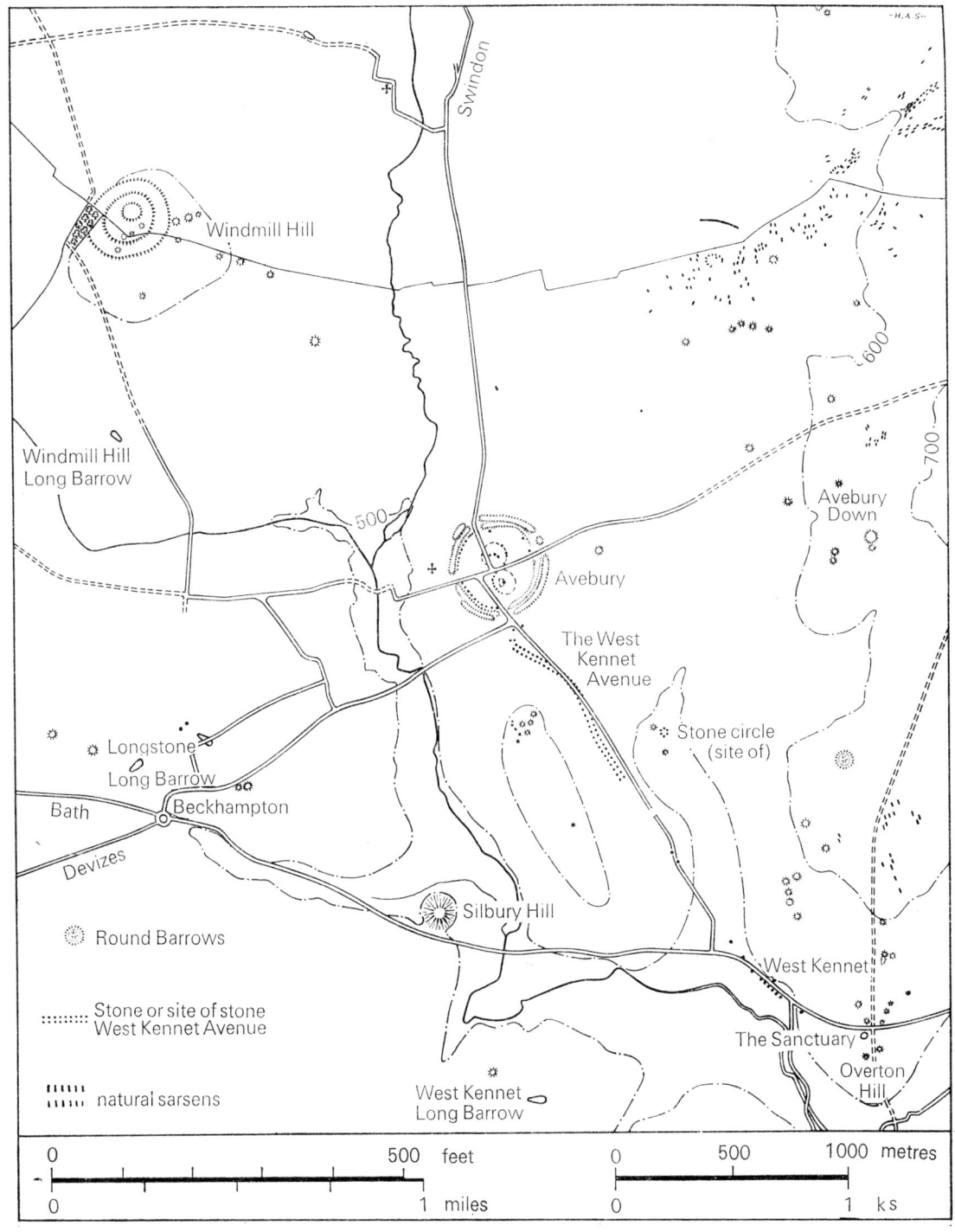

Windmill Hill

Windmill Hill
Long Barrow

Avebury
Down

Avebury

The West
Kennet
Avenue

Stone circle
(site of)

Longstone
Long Barrow

Bath

Beckhampton

Devizes

Silbury Hill

West Kennet

The Sanctuary

Overton
Hill

West Kennet
Long Barrow

⊚ Round Barrows

┈┈ Stone or site of stone
West Kennet Avenue

╷╷╷╷╷ natural sarsens

| 0 | | 500 | feet | | 0 | | 500 | 1000 | metres |

| 0 | | | 1 | miles | | 0 | | | 1 | ks |

Fig 3   *The principal prehistoric monuments of the Avebury region*

rupted at irregular intervals by causeways of undug chalk. In practice the ditches merely served as quarries for material to construct the banks which originally lined the inner lips of the ditches. The outer ditch is the largest and the inner is the slightest. Overall, the enclosed area includes about 20 acres.

A number of causewayed camps are known mainly in the south of England. They are thought to have served as tribal meeting-places inhabited only for a short duration each year. Windmill Hill is one of the best-known examples largely as the result of extensive excavations carried out between 1925-9. The work produced a considerable quantity of archaeological material including implements, pottery and animal bones, all of which are now exhibited in the museum at Avebury.

Other causewayed camps include:

Maiden Castle, lying beneath an Iron Age hill-fort (grid ref. SY667885). There is little to see on the ground but the finds are in the Dorset County Museum at Dorchester.

The *Trundle* near Chichester (grid ref. SU878110). The Neolithic earthworks can be traced quite clearly within the defences of the Iron Age hill-fort.

Whitehawk Hill, north of Brighton, now obscured. The fine collection of material from this excavation is in the Brighton Museum and Art Gallery.

Avebury, *Wiltshire* (grid ref. SU 102700)

Avebury lies on the A361 between Swindon and Devizes. It can also be reached from the A4 by turning on to the A361 at Beckhampton.

Avebury is one of the largest henge monuments now visible. Its most prominent features are a roughly circular enclosing ditch, which in its original form was steep-sided and flat-bottomed, broken by four entrance causeways. The material quarried from the ditch was piled up on the outer edge to create a high bank. On the inner lip of the ditch stood a circle of massive sarsen stones, collected from the neighbouring downs, some of them weighing between 30 and 40 tons. Two different shapes were selected: upright straight-sided stones and diamond-shaped blocks. Originally there would have been about a hundred stones but many of them have since been pulled down and broken up. Inside this Great Circle, which is about 320 ft across, remains of two other circular settings of stones survive.

Avebury is approached by an avenue of standing stones known as the *Kennet Avenue* which runs across country for about a mile to Overton Hill where excavations revealed '*the Sanctuary*', a circular construction built first of timber and later of stone uprights.

The earthworks at Avebury still form an impressive monument. Many of the standing stones in the south-west quadrant have been re-erected and parts of the

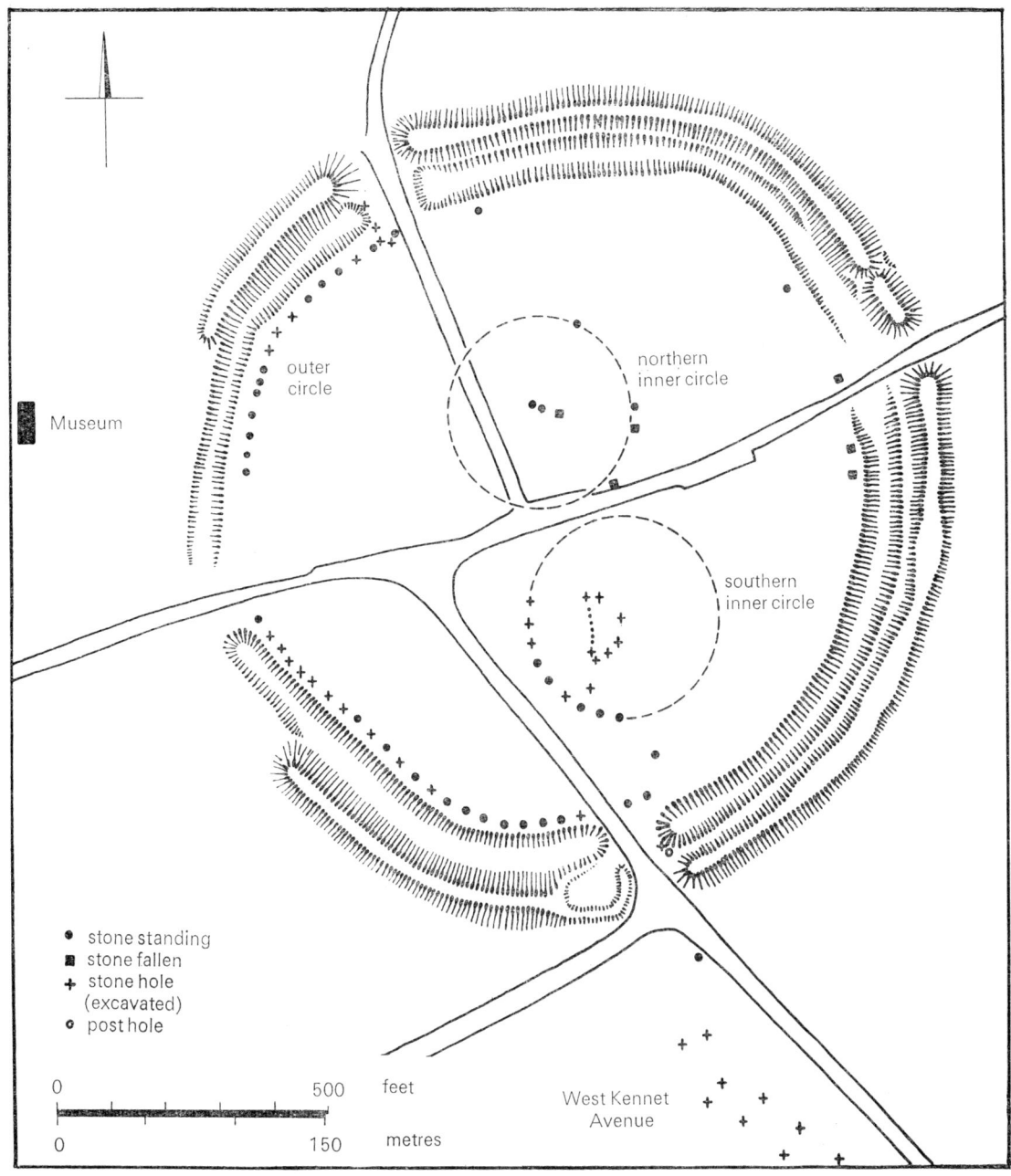

Museum

outer
circle

northern
inner circle

southern
inner circle

- stone standing
- stone fallen
+ stone hole
   (excavated)
∘ post hole

0   500   feet

0   150   metres

West Kennet
Avenue

Fig 4   *Avebury*

Kennet Avenue have been similarly restored. The plan of the Sanctuary has been laid out in the grass with concrete markers. The archaeological material recovered from the excavation of Avebury and the Avenue is now on display in the Avebury Museum: finds from the Sanctuary are in Devizes Museum.

Other stone circles which can still be seen are:

The Knowton Circles, Dorset (grid ref. SU025102)

Stanton Drew, Somerset (grid ref. ST601633)

Another monument of the henge type worth visiting is:

Woodhenge (grid ref. SU 151433) which lies close to the main road from Amesbury to Marlborough (A345) near the much larger henge of Durrington Walls. Woodhenge consisted of six consecutive rows of standing timbers, presumably the uprights of a roofed structure, enclosed by a massive ditch and external bank. The building is similar to that found with the earthworks of Durrington Walls. The positions of the timbers have been indicated on the ground with concrete markers and the archaeological finds from the excavation are on display in Devizes Museum.

Stonehenge, *Wiltshire* (grid ref. SU 122422)

The site lies close to the A344, 3 miles west of Amesbury near the junction with the A303.

Stonehenge is a highly complex monument for which an adequate description cannot be given here. Readers wishing to find out about it in any detail are referred to the books listed on the inside back cover.

The structural history of the site is now well known as the result of a series of recent excavations. In the first period, before 2000 BC, the outer bank and ditch were erected together with the heel stone and probably a wooden gateway nearby. Just inside the bank was a circular setting of small pits (the Aubrey Holes) many of which contained human cremations. Very little is known of any internal buildings but it is not unlikely that a timber structure like the building inside Durrington Walls existed somewhere within the enclosure. In the second period, perhaps about 2000 BC, work began on the erection of a complex stone circle composed of stones derived from the Prescelly Mountains in Pembrokeshire. At this time an avenue, presumably a processional way, defined by banks and ditches, was constructed leading from the banks of the Avon right up to the main entrance to the monument. The blue-stone circle was dismantled in the third period, its place being taken by the massive structure of sarsen stones which forms the dominant feature of the site we see today. In the final stages the blue stones were re-erected on more than one occasion within the sarsen circle.

Stonehenge, then, exhibits a continuity of use and building lasting over many

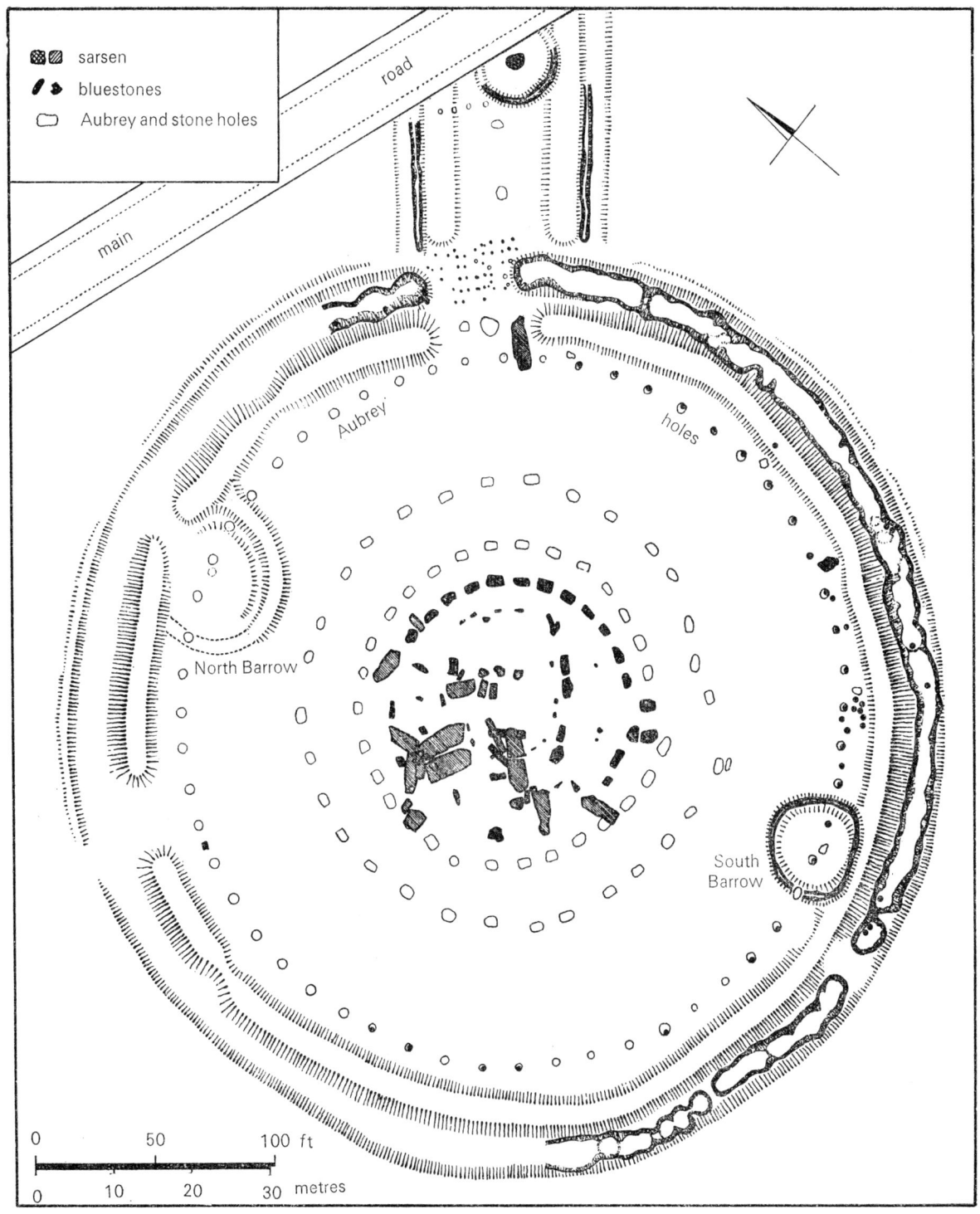

Legend:
- sarsen
- bluestones
- Aubrey and stone holes

road

main

Aubrey

holes

North Barrow

South Barrow

0   50   100 ft

0   10   20   30 metres

Fig 5   Stonehenge

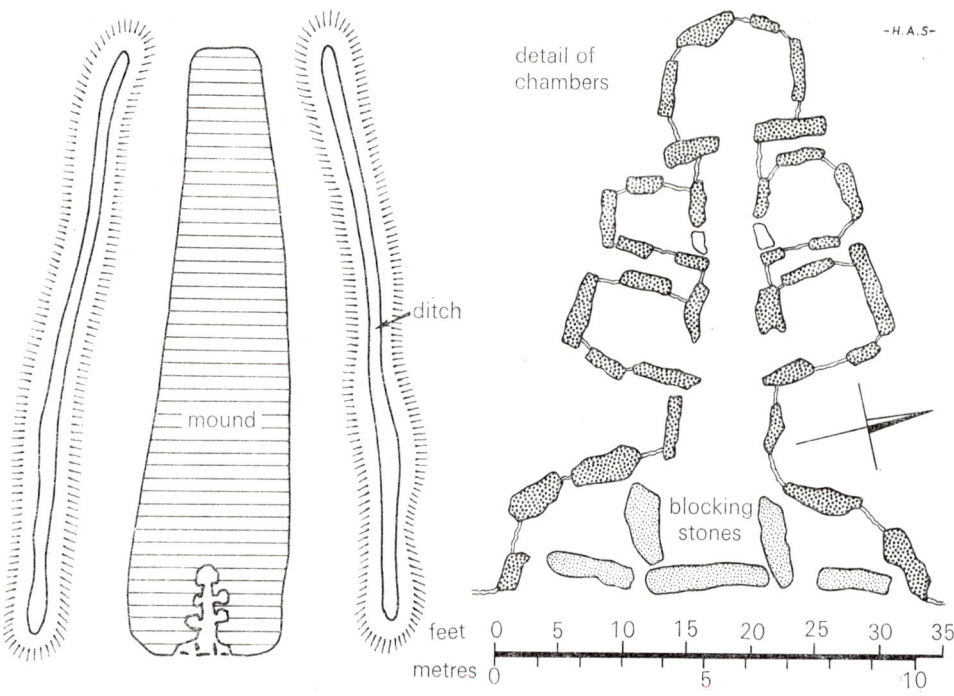

Fig 6   The West Kennet Long Barrow

centuries. Its first phase was similar in many respects to other henge monuments in the country but in its final form it was quite unique.

A model of the monument and the finds from the excavations are exhibited in the Salisbury and South Wilts Museum, Salisbury.

The West Kennet Long Barrow, *Wiltshire* (grid ref. s u 104677)
The barrow can be reached along a footpath leading south from the A4 just west of the village of West Kennet.

The West Kennet Long Barrow is a burial mound built before 2000 b c and used for several centuries. It consists of a mound 350 ft long constructed of chalk quarried out of two flanking ditches and originally curbed with stone boulders. In the east end is set a complex of burial chambers, built with large slabs of sarsen stone, which contained the remains of about thirty bodies deposited over a period of years. When the burial rituals had finally been completed the tomb was sealed with upright stone slabs and dry stone walling.

The tomb is now well displayed to the public: the finds from the excavation are in Devizes Museum.

Avebury, Wiltshire, The 'sacred' area was enclosed by a massive ditch with an external bank, broken by four causeways. Inside were settings of standing stones, a number of which have since been painstakingly re-erected by the archaeologist Alexander Keiller. The ceremonial approach was along an avenue marked by rows of standing stones beside the modern road in the top left of the picture. (see page 12)

Silbury Hill, Wiltshire, is the largest man-made mound in Europe. It looks more massive than it is because the builders chose to construct it on a spur of chalk by digging away the neck of the spur and the area around and piling the soil on to the spur end. Recent excavations have demonstrated how the mound was built but we are unlikely ever to know why. (see page 6)

17

Stonehenge, Wiltshire, is justifiably the most famous of our prehistoric remains. The air view shows very clearly the dark mark of the outer henge-monument ditch dating to before 2000 BC. The final erection of the stones took place after several centuries of alterations and additions; in fact Stonehenge has as complex a building history as the average English Cathedral.
(see page 14)

Snail Down, Wiltshire. This group of barrows is loosely arranged in a linear strip in such a way as to suggest that the cemetery grew in a particular direction. Many of them can be seen to have small pits dug into their centres as the result of barrow robbing carried out during the last century.

'Seven Barrows' on Lambourn Down, Berks. This is another clear example of a barrow cemetery, the barrows now being preserved on a square of unploughed land beyond which recent ploughing has flattened everything. Modern farming methods are fast destroying barrows and there are now relatively few good groups left undamaged.

The Hove Cup. This small, but beautifully-made cup was lathe-turned out of a solid block of amber. It had been placed in a barrow, on the outskirts of Hove, Sussex, sometime about 1600–1700 BC. It is a masterpiece of craftsmanship and must have been exceptionally valuable.
(see page 40)

Gold Mount from Bush Barrow, Wiltshire. Bush Barrow contained an inhumed chieftain buried at about the same time as the Hove Barrow was constructed. Buried with the man was this thin gold fitting (18 cm long). A recent study of the gold objects of this period has suggested that the best of them were made by one craftsman and distributed throughout Wessex. Since gold was extremely valuable it was beaten into thin sheets attached to wood or leather, to make a little metal cover a large area.
(see page 34)

The West Kennet Long Barrow is the best-preserved example of a 'megalithic' tomb in Wessex. The mound was built of chalk dug out of two long side ditches, with a burial chamber of large stone slabs constructed in the East End. For many decades bodies were put into the chambers, earlier burials being cleared away to the sides. Eventually, when the tomb was regarded as full, it was sealed with the massive standing stones which can be seen across the east end.
(see page 16)

A reconstruction of an Iron Age hut at Avoncroft, Warwickshire, based on the ground-plan of one found at the hill-fort of Danes Camp. The most surprising thing that the reconstruction tells us is that the internal volume was more considerable than would have been expected, leaving plenty of space for a loft or for hanging smoked meat.

Celtic fields on Smacam Down, Dorset. Compare the massive lynchets (field banks) on the sloping sides of the valley with the slighter banks on the hilltops where the soil movement would be much less. The regularity of this particular example is a reminder that there must have been times in the past when waste land was systematically cleared and new fields laid out in well-planned order. (see page 45)

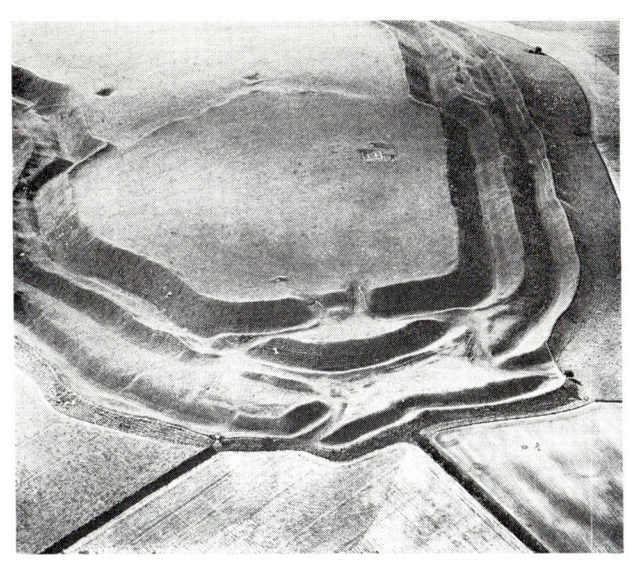

Maiden Castle, Dorset, one of the greatest Iron Age hill-forts of Britain. The bottom view shows very clearly how the whole hillside was sculptured and formed into a series of massive defensive ditches. Originally only the Eastern (right-hand) end of the hill was fortified but later it was more than doubled in area. (The line of the abandoned cross rampart can still be seen.) The two entrances at either end gradually increased in strength as more outworks were added forcing any attacker to wind his way between banks and ditches always under fire from slingers manning artillery platforms. The East gate was eventually attacked and taken by the Roman Second Legion under Vespasian. (see page 56)

The Battersea Shield. One of the most spectacular pieces of Iron Age parade equipment made in the first century AD shortly before the Roman invasion. The shield is of thin bronze originally backed by wood or leather. It would never have been used in battle since it was much too weak, but probably served as part of the display armour of a chieftain. Many elaborate weapons have been found in rivers where they may have been thrown as offerings to the gods.

24

Beacon Hill in North Hampshire. This typical Iron Age hill-fort shows how cleverly the builders followed the contour of the hill so as to take the best advantage of the lie of the land. The disturbed ground inside the defences results largely from the creation of hut platforms contemporary with the defences. Many of the hill-forts were permanently occupied by large communities.

One of the vertebrae belonging to a defender of Maiden Castle when the Romans attacked. He was killed by an iron-tipped ballister bolt (a kind of arrow) which entered his chest and penetrated his spine. After the battle he was buried with the iron point embedded in his back-bone.

Hod Hill, Dorset. Another of the Iron Age hill-forts attacked by the Roman Army in
AD 43. After the fort was taken the Romans established a fort of their own in the corner of
the old defensive circuit. It shows in this photograph as a white area because it had just been
ploughed. It is just possible to make out the lines of the Roman streets within the fort
leading to the Roman gates. (see page 56)

The Roman town of Calleva (Silchester). The line of the town defences, defining a
polygonal area of about 100 acres, show now as lines of trees. Most of the grid of Roman
streets can clearly be seen as light strips in the darker fields. This is because the crop
growing in the thin soil above the thick gravelled streets parched more quickly. A Roman
road leading to the town, partly followed by a modern road, can be seen centre top.
(see page 69)

Reconstruction of the theatre in the Roman town of Verulamium, near St Albans. The theatre lay towards the centre of the town next door to a temple (bottom left). This kind of arrangement was common in the Roman world since the theatre often served as a centre for religious performances connected with temple ritual. (see page 66)

The Gorgons head from Bath. This stone slab occupied a central position in the front of the temple to the goddess Sulis Minerva who presided over the sacred spring in Bath. The Gorgon is normally a female in classical mythology but here is shown as a male with moustaches. Other characteristics of the face are Celtic in inspiration demonstrating a combination of native and Roman ideas. Conflation of this kind was a normal Roman policy when dealing with native gods. (see page 63).

Richborough, Kent. This complex Roman site served as a supply base in the first year or two of the invasion of AD 43, and continued in use into the Saxon period. The cross-shaped mass of masonry is the base of a great triumphal arch, once adorned with marble and bronze statues, put up to commemorate the completion of the conquest of Britain in AD 84. Later in the third century as pirate attacks became more serious, the monument was turned into a lookout post and defended with a system of triple ditches. Finally, late in the third century, the site was enclosed with a wall and ditches to protect a detachment of troops stationed here on the coast to defend the British shores from pirates and invaders.

Portchester Castle, Hampshire. The outer wall, with bastions, was put up in the late third century to house a military contingent similar to that stationed at Richborough. Most of these 'Saxon shore forts' were sited on navigable inlets close to protected anchorages used by the large fleet needed to keep off pirate attack. The walls of Portchester continued to be used by the Saxons and throughout the medieval period.

All of these late Roman forts were defended by forward projecting bastions which would have served as fighting platforms. This bastion at Portchester may once have supported a piece of artillery capable of hurling stones or volleys of arrows at attackers.

The signs of affluence and luxury which appealed to the owners of the rich Roman villas were mosaics, baths and central heating. At the villa at Bignor, Sussex, one of the rooms was adorned with a floor depicting cupids acting as gladiators. The figure on the right is the training instructor.

At Lullingstone, in Kent, the main room was provided with this fine figured floor incorporating a scene from the legend of Bellerophon slaying the Chimara. Mythical scenes were popular among the rich.

At Chedworth, Gloucestershire, a simpler geometric mosaic can be seen supported on pilae (stacks of tiles) arranged so as to create a hollow space (hypocaust) beneath the floor through which hot air would circulate to heat the room.

2. Metal Workers and Traders

Sometime just before 2000 BC a completely new technological development was introduced into Britain from the continent – the knowledge of extracting and working metal. To begin with the metal used was copper, but it was soon found that a better cutting edge could be produced by adding tin to make the alloy bronze. After a period of experiment, the ideal proportions of the two metals were found to be about 11 per cent tin to 89 per cent copper which yielded a bronze that was both easy to cast and strong in use. Metal extraction was a major breakthrough not least because the development of the actual techniques involved would have required abstract thought and a considerable range of experiment before the processes were perfected sufficiently to be passed on from one generation to the next. The production of a simple bronze axe needed a wide range of skills. First of all the ores of copper and tin had to be discovered and dug out, then the metal had to be extracted by processes first of roasting to produce the oxide and then reduction in a carefully controlled atmosphere at a high temperature. Next the metals had to be mixed in the correct proportions and melted down before the resulting alloy could be cast into stone or clay moulds to produce the rough cast object. Finally would have come the processes of trimming, beating out a cutting edge, and sharpening.

To begin with metal was rare and no doubt expensive. It was used sparingly for small objects and trinkets alongside the more common stone tools, but as production increased and more and more metal came on to the market, weapons and, later, general-purpose tools were all made in bronze. By about 1000 BC the industry was firmly established on a sound economic basis. All parts of the country would have been served by itinerant bronze smiths moving about their territories from one community to another, prepared to make implements or weapons on demand in exchange for food or scrap metal, just like the tinkers of the last century. There were, too, far more accomplished craftsmen working in the west of Britain from 900 to 500 BC who were capable of making fine cauldrons and buckets of beaten bronze sheets riveted together. In the same areas display shields of beaten bronze were produced and more rarely musical wind instruments known as lurers. These craftsmen, unlike the tinkers, were probably working for the luxury market making consumer goods which only the upper class could afford.

Although bronze-working technology established itself rapidly in Britain, its initial introduction appears to have been the result of an influx of new people from the continent. These people are referred to by archaeologists as the 'Beaker Folk' because of a characteristic vessel which they frequently buried with their dead. Recent research has shown that the movements of people about the European mainland and Britain are far more complex than we originally believed, and we must now assume that the period from about 2200 to 1600 BC saw a considerable mobility during which the indigenous population was augmented by new immigrants bringing with them new skills and a somewhat different ideology.

The different beliefs of the 'Beaker Folk' are best exemplified by contrasting their burials with the collective tombs of the indigenous population. Typically, a 'Beaker' burial consists of a single crouched inhumation laid in a shallow grave cut into the bedrock. Frequently a decorated beaker was placed with the body, sometimes close to the hands as if it had been clasped by the deceased. Less often, personal trinkets are found such as beads, a bronze or copper knife and a whetstone for sharpening it. The male burials were probably provided with bows and arrows, but the only traces which occasionally survive are flint arrowheads and the stone wrist guard which an archer would wear to protect his left wrist from the bowstring. The typical 'Beaker' burial, then, emphasised the individual and his need to maintain his individuality by taking his personal equipment with him to the afterlife. The contrast with the collective burial of the earlier population is dramatic.

It is difficult to say what effect the immigrants and their ideology had on the development of the great ritual monuments, but where evidence survives 'Beaker' material can sometimes be shown to be associated with the stone circles and alignments. It is therefore probable that the staggering intellectual advances implied by these structures owe much to the new people.

Although, as we have seen, a class structure was evident in the burial rituals before 2000 BC, it becomes far more noticeable in the following 500 years with the appearance, in central southern England, of a group of immensely rich burials, placed centrally beneath barrows sometimes of considerable proportions. These were the graves of the rich, and no doubt powerful, men and women who, by virtue of their acquired or inherited power, must have been able to control society in such a way as to accumulate the surpluses of the common people for themselves. There is no longer any need to think of these chieftains as a foreign hierarchy, rather they are the product of a merging of the indigenous and 'Beaker' populations. This came about at a time when the acquisition of individual wealth was being made easier by the exploitation of the new range of exotic materials brought on to the market by technological advance stimulated by demand.

We have only to look at the famous burial from Bush Barrow, near Wilsford in Wiltshire, to see these theoretical points made evident. The chieftain here was provided with an axe head, two (or three) daggers, one of which had a wooden

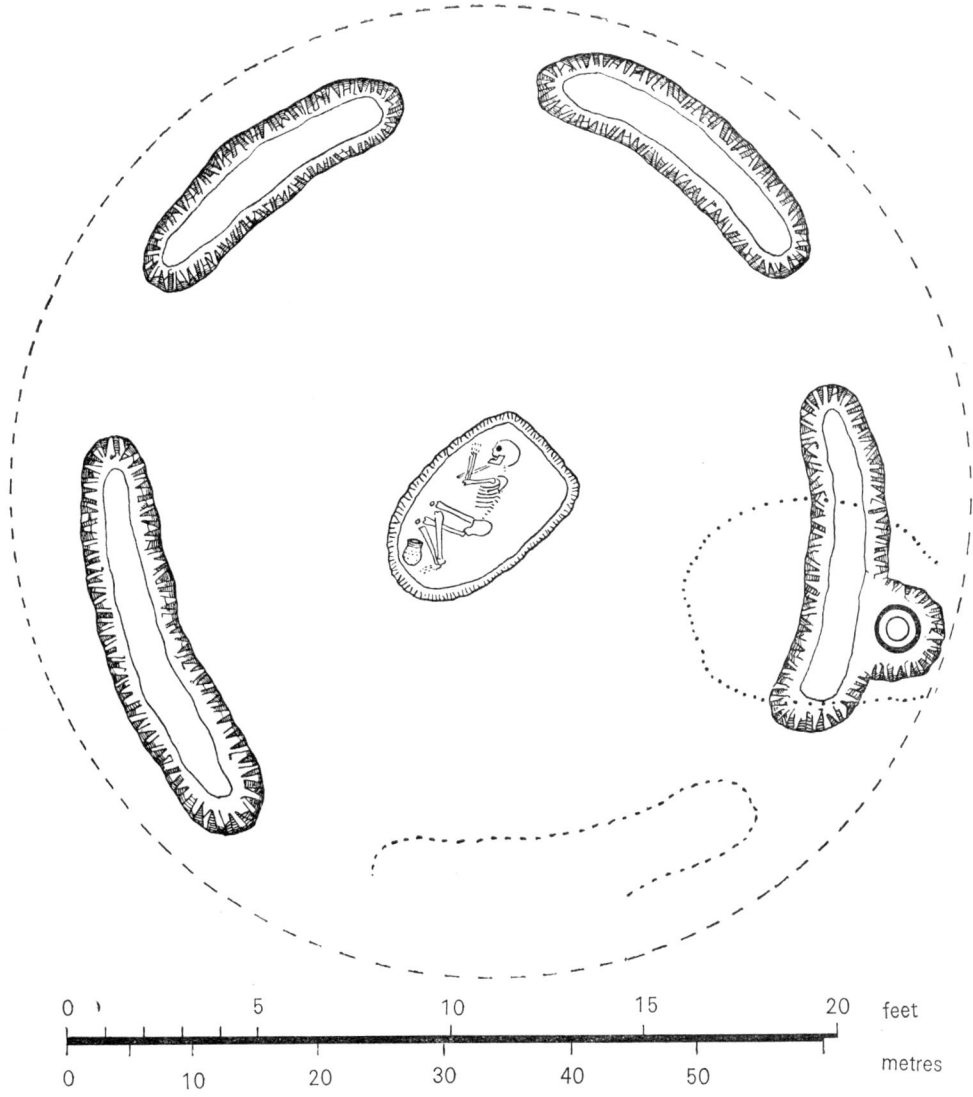

| 0 | | 5 | | 10 | | 15 | | 20 | feet |
| 0 | | 10 | | 20 | | 30 | | 40 | | 50 | | metres |

Fig 7   Beaker burial on Stockbridge Down, Hants

haft inset with hundreds of small gold pins, a mace head of rare fossiliferous stone from Devon, a wooden sceptre decorated with zigzag bone rings, and three plaques of gold, all elaborately decorated and once attached to his clothing. His daggers presumably demonstrate his prestige as a warrior, while the sceptre and mace must symbolise authority. The fact that he could afford so much gold can only be regarded as an indication of his wealth.

The gold and mace head arrived in Wiltshire as a result of trade along with a whole range of other exotic materials including the blue, glassy faience beads, amber used for beads and other ornaments, and occasionally for making vessels,

35

and shale from Kimmeridge Bay in Dorset, which was made into cups, beads and sometimes used as a backing material for gold. We must also remember that there may have been a lively trade in less durable things like furs, fabrics and spices, but no trace of this can be expected to survive in the archaeological record. The organisational effort involved in the discovery, exploitation and distribution of these exotic materials for the aristocratic market, together with a no less impressive effort behind the trade in bronzes, must mean that a number of specialists were now employed full-time in non-food-producing activities. These specialists must therefore have been supported by society's surplus. If we assume that the food-producing capacity of the land is not likely to have changed substantially in the thousand years between 2500 and 1500 BC, then we are forced to conclude that much of the surplus which had once been invested in the construction of the great communal monuments was now channelled into the production of luxury goods for the upper classes. In other words, society's productive energies were now being exploited for the benefit of a few individuals.

A system such as this had some positive advantages. Demand for quantities of good bronze gradually cheapened the metal so that weapons and tools soon came within the range of most people in the community, while the growing aristocratic market for objects of display provided a system within which craftsmen could work under the patronage of the rich. A recent study of much of the Wessex gold has suggested that it was, in fact, the work of a single skilled artist. Similarly, no one looking at the exquisite amber cup found in a burial at Hove could doubt that it was produced by a craftsman of very considerable accomplishment.

The changes which came about in society after about 1600 BC are difficult to assess in any detail, partly because burial ritual changed to become almost exclusively cremation. Cremation had been practised from time to time before 2200 BC, but the incursions of the 'Beaker' people, who normally inhumed their dead, tended to overshadow native developments for a few centuries until they gradually became dominant again. The ashes of the dead were placed in urns and either buried beneath barrows or inserted into existing ones. Since cremation burial leaves little trace of the objects with which the dead person may have been accompanied on the funeral pyre, it is difficult to compare the wealth and class structure of the period 1500 to 500 BC with the preceding thousand years, but the general impression to be gained from what little evidence exists is that differences between rich and poor burials became less until, towards the end of the period, everyone was buried simply in a flat grave in a series of large cemeteries or urnfields. This does not, of course, necessarily reflect a levelling-out of social differences: it may mean no more than that views on the afterlife changed and people lost interest in elaborate burial procedures.

Evidence from settlement sites and surviving bronze objects tend, however, to support the idea that the pace of life had slowed down. The period of glossy display was over and, apart from minor improvements, technological advances were no longer being made. Even the great ritual monuments had ceased to be used. In fact, after the centuries of innovation, British society had settled down to a period of mundane conservatism.

From about the eighth century BC significant changes become apparent. It seems that Britain began once more to develop widespread contacts with all parts of Europe, leading to the importation and trading of luxury goods such as buckets and cauldrons as well as horse trappings and possibly horses. These were the equipment of an heroic, wine-drinking aristocracy of the kind which is known to have been developing at this time on the continent. The appearance of these trappings, whether accompanied by people or not, marks the beginning of a new aggressive trend in the social development of the country.

SITES TO VISIT

Several of the monuments described on pages 10-16 continued in use throughout the early part of the period considered in this section. The stones at *Avebury* and the *West Kennet Avenue* are associated with 'Beaker' remains, and the second phase of *Stonehenge*, the blue stone circle, is also of this period, while its third phase overlaps in time with the chieftains' burials of Wessex. Even the old collective tomb at *West Kennet* was used to house a 'Beaker' burial.

The most characteristic field monuments of this period are the round barrows which occur in vast numbers all over the south of Britain. Many of them are marked as 'tumuli' on Ordnance Survey maps. Three groups have been selected for brief description below largely because they are readily accessible by road and contain exceptionally well-preserved examples of the various different types.

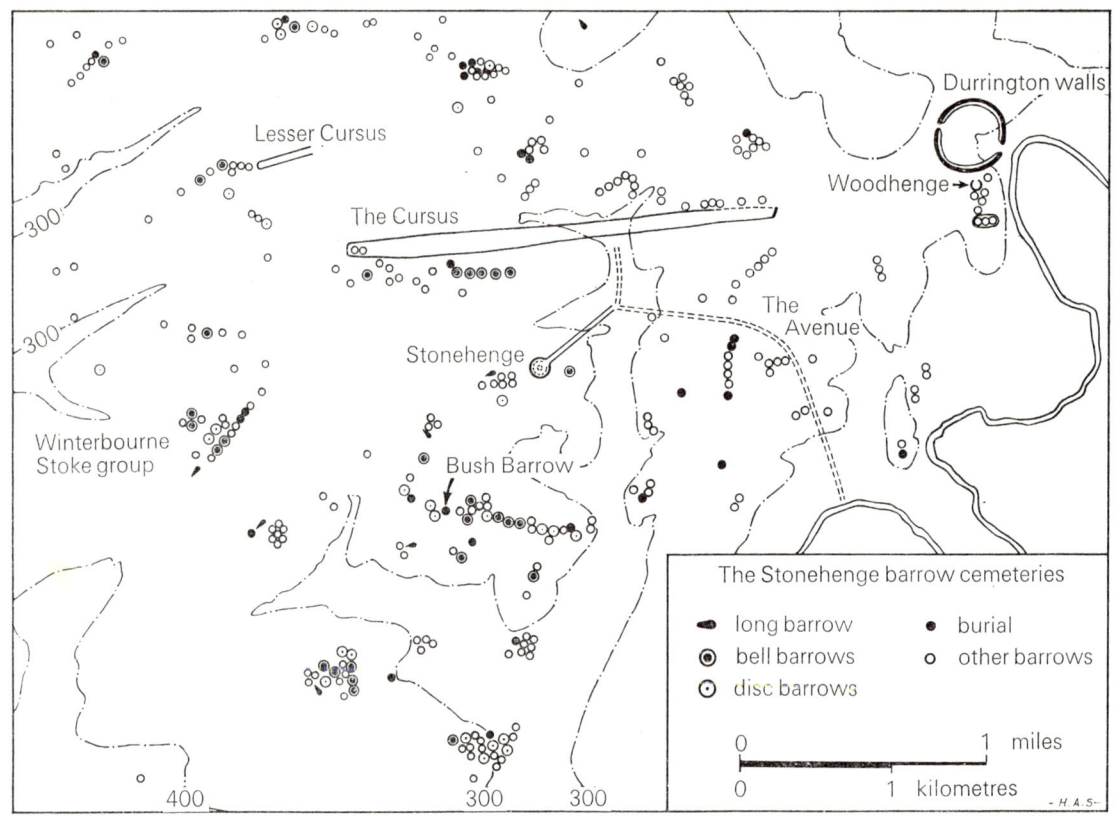

Fig 8   The prehistoric monuments in the Stonehenge region

Winterbourne Stoke Cross Roads, *Wiltshire* (grid ref. SU100416)

This group lies on the A303 about one and a half miles south-west of Stonehenge.

Like many groups of barrows, most of the examples here are arranged in a linear fashion as though they were built along an ancient track. The oldest barrow is the earthen long barrow probably belonging to the period 3000 to 2500 B C, but the remainder are all round barrows dating from *c.* 2200 – 1600 B C. Three major types are represented: (a) simple *bowl barrows* consisting of circular mounds with a ditch running round the edge of the mound; (b) *bell barrows* which are usually larger, the mound being separated from the ditch by a flat berm; (c) *disc barrows* which consist of a small mound above the burial set within a circular enclosure bounded by a ditch and internal bank.

In general terms, the bowl barrows are found to cover burials of the 'Beaker' period, while the bell and disc barrows usually house the later aristocratic burials quite often with males in the bell barrows and females in the disc barrows.

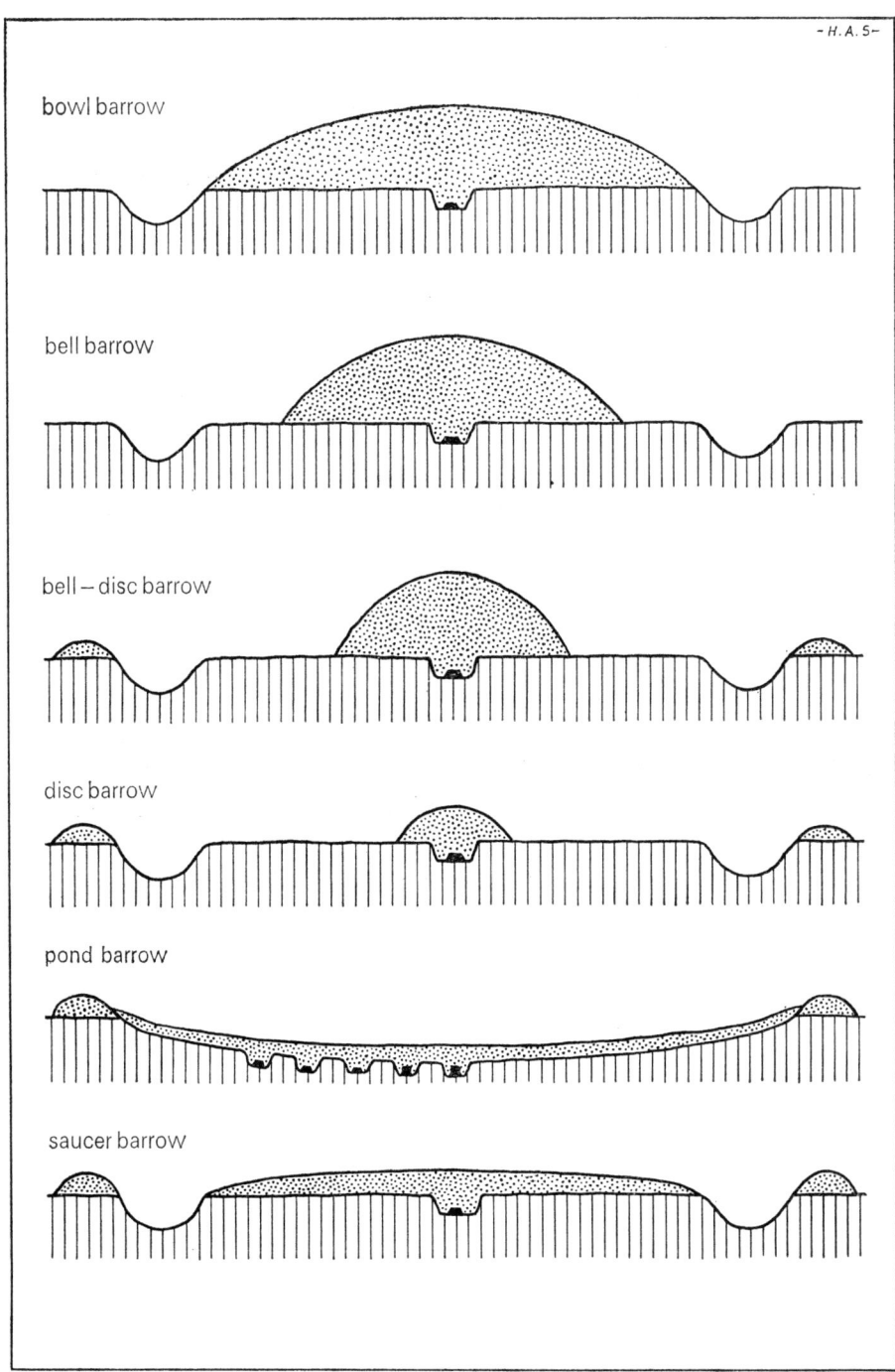

bowl barrow

bell barrow

bell – disc barrow

disc barrow

pond barrow

saucer barrow

Fig 9   Types of bronze age barrows seen in section

Oakley Down, *Dorset* (grid ref. su019173)

This group lies largely to the east of the A354, 12 miles south of Salisbury.

A wide range of different types are represented here including bowl barrows, bell barrows and six disc barrows, some of which are unusual in that they contain two small mounds within a single enclosing ditch of oval plan. One barrow of this type has been partly truncated by the Roman road from Old Sarum to Badbury, which survives as a massive agger along the eastern edge of the barrow group.

Kingston Russell, *Dorset* (grid ref. sy590908)

On either side of the A35 between Bridport and Dorchester, which in this area runs along the line of an ancient track known as the South Dorset ridgeway, is a remarkable series of barrows stretching for miles. The group at Poor Lot, half a mile south-east of Kingston Russell, is particularly impressive. Practically every type of barrow is represented, including a twin bell barrow and a triple bowl barrow. Altogether 44 individual barrows are recorded in this group.

Many of the barrows of southern Britain have been excavated and the finds from them have usually found their way into local museums. The most comprehensive collections are in Devizes Museum, the Salisbury and South Wiltshire Museum, Salisbury, and the Dorset County Museum in Dorchester. Most of the gold objects from the rich chieftains' barrows are now in the British Museum. Other local and county museums often contain important objects or collections, e.g. the famous Hove amber cup which is now in the Brighton Museum and Art Gallery.

3. Man and the Land

The great advances in technology and architecture, and the dramatic changes in social structure which we have considered in the previous sections, could only have come about in a society which produced more food than its members needed to stay alive. The production of a surplus above the needs of subsistence was always a desirable aim and, to judge by the amount of man-power available for building the great ritual monuments of the neolithic period, this aim must have been realised very early on in Man's farming history.

The exact pattern of agricultural activity before 2000 B C is somewhat obscure. Land was being cleared of its forest. This much is recognisable by studying the changes in the pollen sequences preserved in bogs and in fossil turf-lines sealed by later earthworks. Recent excavations have also brought to light plough marks belonging to this period, surviving now as furrows scoring the bedrock. The cereals grown included wheat in large quantities and lesser percentages of a simple form of barley, both known from actual cereal grains which survive either because they were charred or because they became embedded in the fabric of pottery and can be recognised now as casts. Rather small straggly cows and sheep were kept as well as some goats, and pigs were eaten in quantity but whether they were mainly hunted or domesticated is at present open to some doubt. We must also remember that the food supply was regularly augmented by hunting deer of various types and collecting shellfish, eggs and a wide range of nutritious plants. In a good year, with careful husbandry, food must have been plentiful and life stable.

The story of British agriculture over the next 2000 years is one of gradual improvement and adaptation until, at the time of Caesar's invasions in 55 and 54 B C, Britain was productive enough to export corn and Caesar could record that 'the population is exceedingly large, the ground thickly studded with homesteads and the cattle very numerous'.

Changes in the agricultural pattern are not always easy to trace archaeologically; a great deal more work needs to be done on the subject but the general trends are becoming clearer. What we know least about is the nature of the balance between cereal growing and stock rearing. The two practices were, of course, closely intertwined; stock wandering over fields would manure the ground while the stubble left after cropping would provide food for the animals. Some archaeologists believe that during the time when the Beaker settlers were moving in (c. 2200–1600) there was a definite shift of emphasis towards a rather more pastoral type of economy. If so, one contributory cause may have been that after 2000 years of exploitation the land was becoming exhausted and crops were beginning to fail. Whether or not this eventually proves to be true it must always be remembered that primitive agricultural techniques must have turned much rich land into waste for hundreds of years at a time and forced communities to move or adapt.

From about 1500 BC until the Roman Conquest the picture becomes much clearer and it is possible to recognise the emergence of well-established farmsteads, or hamlets, lying among acres of small squarish fields, generally, if inaccurately, referred to as 'celtic fields'. A careful study of any typical piece of chalk downland, where sufficient traces survive modern agricultural activity, often shows areas of ancient arable land spreading out around settlements and giving way to hill-top pastures sometimes provided with ditched enclosures for collecting and corralling livestock. Trackways leading between fields and from one settlement to another were a common feature of the landscape and in some areas linear banks and ditches often running for miles across the countryside served to divide up one territory from another. There can be little doubt that during this period the landscape was becoming progressively more organised as more land was cleared and farming methods became better adapted to the limits imposed by the environment.

The prehistoric farming year can be reconstructed from the archaeological remains. Ploughing was carried out with a simple wooden ard, the point of which was sometimes, in the later period, tipped with a shoe of iron to prevent it from wearing away. The ard differed from a proper plough in that, since it had no mould board for turning the sod, it could only scratch furrows through the soil. For this reason it seems that the fields had to be ploughed twice, the second time at right angles to the first, so as to break up the soil thoroughly enough for sowing. The means of traction, as in the medieval period, was probably a pair of oxen yoked together.

Fig 10 Ard (light plough) of the kind used in the iron age

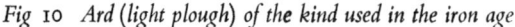

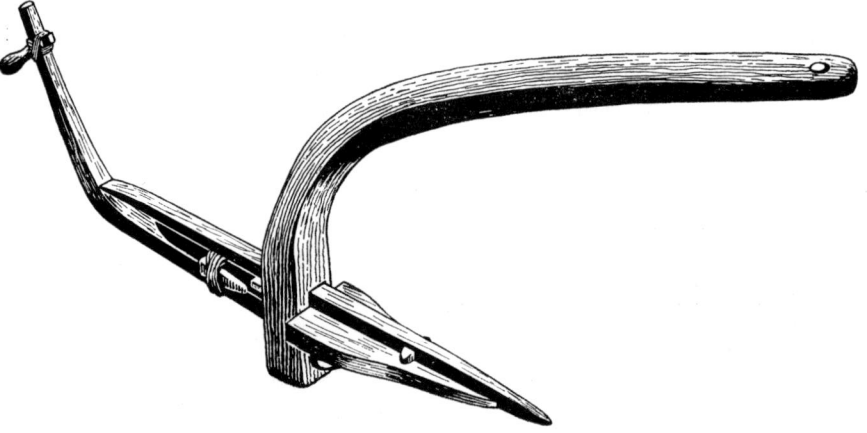

Most of the sowing took place in the spring, but sometime between 1000–500 BC two new types of winter-sown grain were introduced, a wheat called einkorn and a husked barley. This was a distinct improvement because it meant that not only could the effort of ploughing and sowing now be spread out, but also that the period of harvesting was lengthened, the winter-sown crop ripening earlier. For communities whose main problem was eking out their food during the winter, early cropping would have been a tremendous advantage. The grain was harvested, using small reaping hooks made of bronze and later of iron, probably by cutting off the ears high on the stalks and leaving the straw in the fields. If harvesting was carried out before the crop was thoroughly ripe the straw would have retained sufficient goodness to make it worth turning cattle loose in the fields.

The ears of corn were carried back to the farmstead, dried, threshed and stored. Two types of storage methods were used: the grain was either stacked in timber granaries with raised floors or was tipped into large pits. Storage in underground silos was not practised on any scale until 500–300 BC, but after this time it became very popular and settlements of the later period are found to be peppered with large numbers of these storage pits, often many hundreds of them. The pits would have been sealed until the corn was required and then a temporary cover put over the one in use so that the grain could be taken out as and when the community needed it. It was then ground on quern stones into a coarse flour for baking or for making into a gruel.

Animals played a vital part in the economy not only as a ready supply of meat but also as providers of traction, manure and raw materials like bone, hide and wool. Throughout most of the prehistoric period Man was a beef-eater but at certain times, particularly during the two or three hundred years before the Roman invasion, sheep became very numerous, although in terms of sheer volume of meat, mutton consumption probably never exceeded that of beef. Pork was always popular but as forest cover decreased with the advance of cultivated land there was progressively less woodland to provide pannage for large herds of swine. Looking after animals throughout the winter was always a problem for early rural communities. Gradually, after the autumn gleaning among the stubble, the animals would have had to be brought in close to the homestead and throughout the winter watered and fed with hay, straw and leaf fodder. The older animals were killed off as the winter progressed and their meat was salted or smoked and probably hung up in the rafters of the hut until required. Then in the spring the over-wintered beasts were turned loose in the pastures and the fallow fields to crop the new growth of grass.

The routine of farming life was simple and well established. In an average year life, though hard, must have been comfortable, but if the harvest was a failure or the livestock suffered from an epidemic a community could be reduced to starvation level within a few months. Prehistoric life must always have been precarious.

The average farmstead was largely self-supporting. Wool was spun into yarn, dyed with vegetable dyes and woven into fabrics on upright looms. Leather was cured, tanned and made up into clothing and containers, while animal bones were fashioned into a wide range of useful tools as well as into ornaments. Carpentry and basketry were also practised on a considerable scale. Some materials could not be locally produced. Metals, for example, had to be extracted by specialists and traded to the farms by tinkers but after iron became popular sometime about 500 BC the bronze smiths gradually went out of business. Iron was, after all, far easier to extract and to work than bronze and there is some evidence to suggest that it may have been worked by the farming communities themselves, although by the second century BC it seems that iron bars, presumably produced by specialists, were being traded to the rural population for them to forge locally.

Gradually specialisation increased. Pottery manufacture, which for thousands of years had been largely a home craft, began to be taken over by commercial producers from about the fourth century BC, each centre supplying a well-defined local market area with its better-quality 'table ware' for use alongside home-made cooking vessels. Other desirable raw materials, more restricted in their distribution, were also extracted and traded by specialists. Salt, for example, always a vital commodity, was produced along the coast by the evaporation of sea water, the salt cake being packed into clay containers for transportation to inland sites. Fragments of these containers have been found on sites 40-50 miles from the sea. One of the principle salt-producing areas, Kimmeridge Bay on the Dorset coast, also provided another sought-after material – a black shiny shale which for hundreds of years was dug out of the cliffs and carried to neighbouring farmsteads, there to be carved into beautifully polished bracelets. These bracelets and sometimes the raw shale itself were traded to all parts of southern Britain.

Throughout much of the time covered by these developments the basic unit of habitation was the isolated farm set in its farmyard and surrounded by fields. Occasionally several homesteads seem to have grown up close together representing, perhaps, the extended family, that is the married children setting up house close to their parents. Details of kinship and tenurial rites are, however, beyond the scope of the archaeological evidence to discover.

Massive architectural works like the causewayed camps and the henge monuments ceased to be used after about 1600 but there is some evidence that communal structures in the form of large plateau enclosures were erected and maintained as centres for tribal meetings, at least into the middle of the first millen-

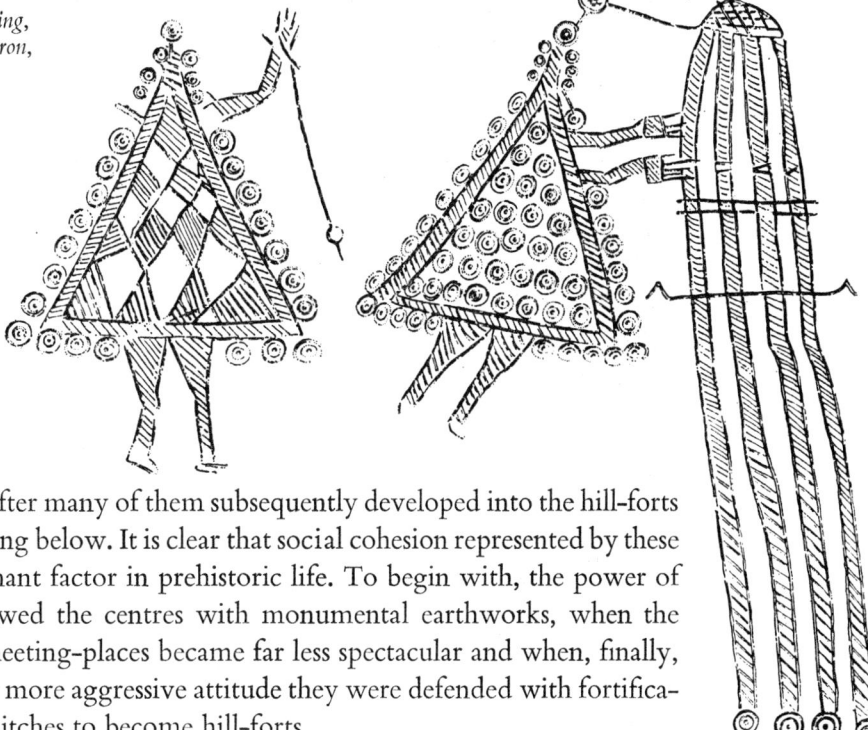

Fig 11 Representation of women weaving and spinning, incised on pottery from Sopron, Hungary

nium BC, and thereafter many of them subsequently developed into the hill-forts we shall be considering below. It is clear that social cohesion represented by these centres was a dominant factor in prehistoric life. To begin with, the power of the theocracy endowed the centres with monumental earthworks, when the power waned the meeting-places became far less spectacular and when, finally, society took on a far more aggressive attitude they were defended with fortifications of banks and ditches to become hill-forts.

SITES TO VISIT

Celtic Fields

The name celtic fields is applied to rectangular plots of land usually defined by lynchet banks or stone walls, which were formed at any time during the prehistoric and Roman period. Vast systems of celtic fields, covering many hundreds of acres, once survived in southern Britain but modern farming methods are fast obliterating them. Characteristically celtic fields were small and squarish or rectangular in plan. Their boundaries were formed in a variety of ways. After the initial clearing of the land, fences or drystone walls may have been erected. Following the first few ploughings stones would have been cleared off the land and thrown around the edges, creating banks. If the field was on a slope, continual ploughing would gradually have encouraged the loosened soil to move down the slope of the field to bank up at the extremity of ploughing in the form of a

Fig 12 Stages in the formation of a lynchet

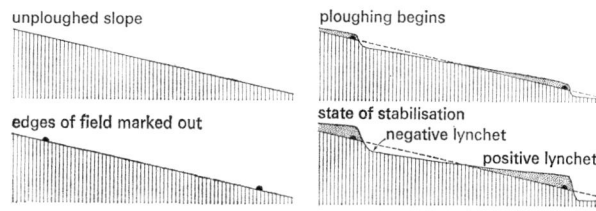

unploughed slope

ploughing begins

edges of field marked out

state of stabilisation

negative lynchet

positive lynchet

positive lynchet. Conversely, the hollowing which would occur at the upper edge is called a *negative lynchet.* In a system of adjacent fields the positive lynchet of one field and the negative lynchet of an adjacent one would create a very considerable change in level. Good examples of field systems together with their trackways, boundary ditches and adjacent settlements can be seen in many parts of the country. They are best viewed in early morning or late evening when the sun is low and the banks cast long shadows. A selection of the better examples include:

Winterbourne Steepleton, Dorset (grid ref. SY 598875)
Chaldon Herring, Dorset (grid ref. SY 795805)
Kingston Down, Dorset (grid ref. SY 957780)
Fyfield Down, Wiltshire (grid ref. SU 140710)

Little Woodbury, Wiltshire (grid ref. SU 150279)
Little Woodbury, 2 miles south of Salisbury, is one of the best-known settlement sites in southern Britain but nothing remains to be seen on the ground. Nevertheless extensive excavations before the war brought to light all the main features of a farmstead dating to the period 400-100 BC.

The farm buildings were surrounded by an enclosure, originally of timber but later replaced by a bank and ditch. The single gate was linked to a series of radiat-

Fig 13   *Celtic fields at Chaldon Herring and West Lulworth*

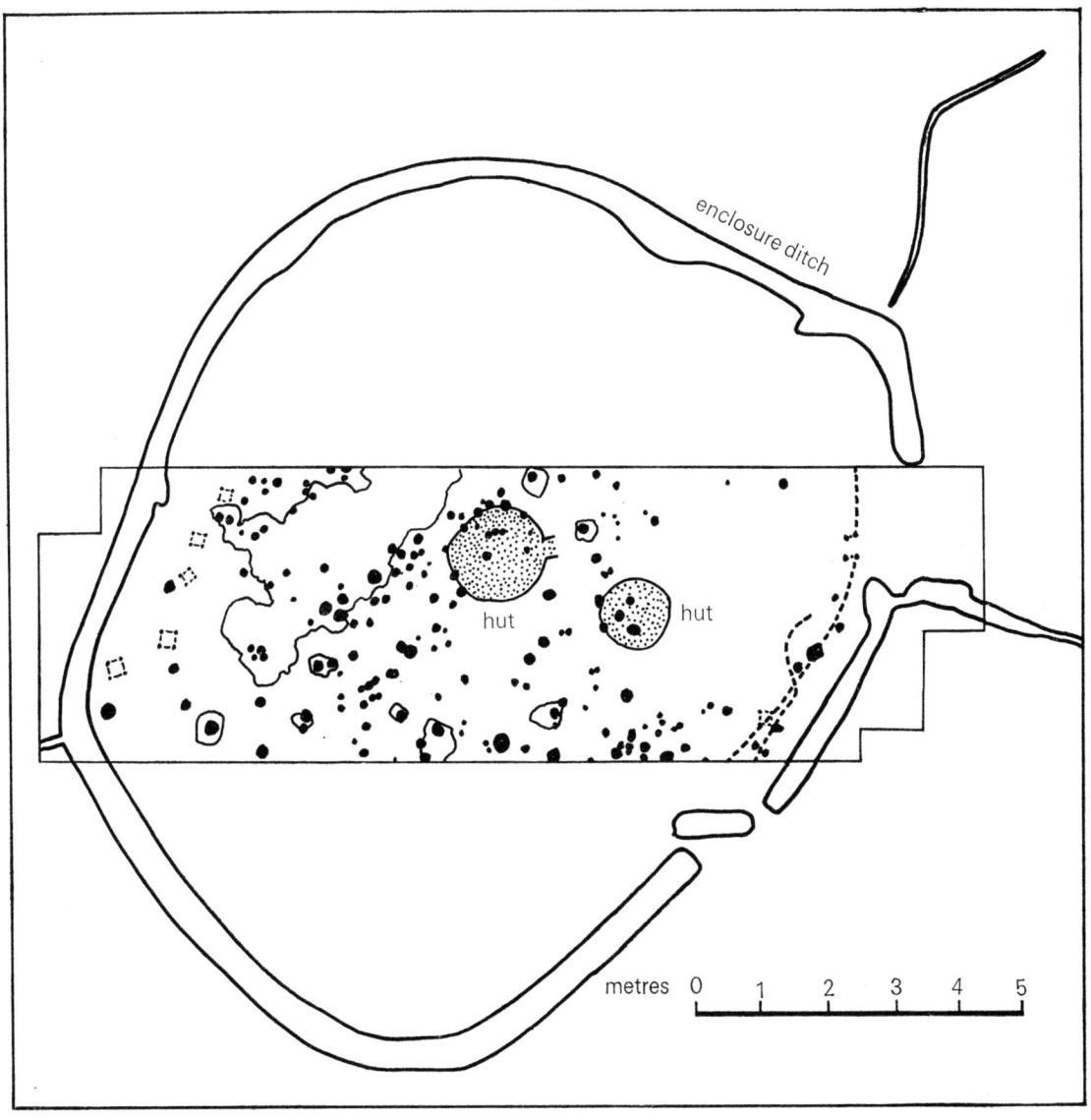

Fig 14 *Little Woodbury*

ing ditches which may have been designed to make it easier to drive the stock towards the enclosure at times when they needed to be collected together. Within the enclosure two houses were found but they were thought not to be contemporary. Since only part of the defended area was excavated, the possibility remains of other houses still undiscovered. The largest house was a massive structure with its roof supported on a circle of upright timbers, the rafters extending beyond them to an outer wall so as to create a circular space around the central area, useful as storage or sleeping quarters. The entrance was built in the form

47

of a long passage presumably with an inner and outer door to exclude draughts.

In the farm-yard around the house all the basic activities of the community were carried out. Corn was probably dried in the 'working hollow', storage pits occurred in large numbers, while settings of four posts may well represent above-ground granaries. Pairs of post holes also turn up but the function is uncertain; possibly they supported hay racks or looms. As to the rest of the post holes, they may have resulted from a range of activities – from pegging out skins for drying to tethering animals.

Little Woodbury may prove to be an exceptional site in the intensity of its occupation and the complexity of its main hut when we have more settlements with which to compare it, but at present it may be taken to symbolise one of the basic units of farming economy in the late first millennium BC.

Hundreds of other homesteads of the period from 1500 to the Roman Conquest exist all over the south of Britain but without exception there is little to be seen save for a few earthworks in those exceptional cases where modern ploughing has not obliterated all surface trace. Further west on Dartmoor and Bodmin Moor, clear of modern agriculture, settlement remains survive in better order but description of them is beyond the scope of the present work.

Reconstruction and Experiment

To test their hypothesis about early methods of agriculture and construction some archaeologists are now beginning to carry out experiments. The experiments are usually short-lived and leave little to see but two locations deserve further mention:

Avoncroft, *Worcestershire* (grid ref. SO 950681)

Avoncroft houses an open-air museum of buildings. One corner of the site is devoted to the full-scale reconstruction of a farm of about 200 BC, which includes a stone-walled circular hut based on the ground plan of one excavated at Danes Camp, Worcestershire, and a wattle and daub hut like those found at Glastonbury in Somerset. Both huts are set within a ditched enclosure, backed by a palisade. Experiments in weaving, grain storage and the cultivation of primitive wheat are also being carried out.

Butser Hill, *Hampshire* (grid ref. SU 715205)

An ancient farm is soon to be established on Butser Hill as part of a project to study a wide range of problems connected with primitive agriculture. The farm will be built close to the site of an actual settlement of the 5th-3rd century. Butser Hill possesses a number of ancient earthworks including a series of dykes which delimit a plateau enclosure of the type mentioned above, as well as the bank and ditch of an unfinished hill-fort.

4. Aggression

As the period of the Roman invasion approaches, our knowledge of the people of Britain improves. No longer do we have to rely entirely upon the fragmentary archaeological evidence to study them, for now the literate classical world has at last made contact with these northern barbarians whom they describe with evident fascination. First by hearsay, later by contact through direct trading missions, and finally by conquest, the Romans discovered the Britons:

'The people who live by the promontory . . . called Belerium (Cornwall) are remarkably friendly and through close contact with foreign traders are fairly civilised.' (Diodorus)

'The men are taller than the Gauls and their hair is not so yellow; and they are more loosely-made . . . At Rome we saw certain British youths who were half a foot taller than the tallest there; but they were bandy-legged and rather clumsily built in general.' (Strabo)

'By far the most civilised inhabitants are those living in Kent . . . All the Britons dye their bodies with woad, which produces a blue colour, and this gives then a more terrifying appearance in battle. They wear their hair long and shave the whole of their bodies except the head and upper lip. Wives are shared between groups of ten or twelve men, especially between brothers and between fathers and sons; but the offspring of these unions are counted as the children of the man with whom a particular woman cohabited first.' (Caesar)

Several writers stress the close similarities between the Britons and the society of the other Celtic tribes of Europe with whom they were in close contact. It seems that the Celts were developing distinctly flamboyant and aggressive tendencies: they were, in fact, becoming an heroic society in which daring exploits were a status symbol. Raiding, fighting and boasting became a way of life and great feasts at which these deeds would be proclaimed and discussed were central to the whole pattern of existence. The Celts had become, as one classical writer remarked, 'war-mad'.

When Julius Caesar made his abortive raids on Britain in 55 and 54 BC he immediately came up against the military strength of the people: 'In chariot fighting they began by driving all over the field hurling javelins and generally the terror inspired by the horses and the noise of the wheels are sufficient to throw their opponents' ranks into disorder. Then, after making their way between the squadrons of their own cavalry they jump down from the chariots and engage on foot. In the meantime their charioteers retire a short distance from the battle and place the chariots in such a position that their masters, if hard pressed by numbers, have an easy means of retreat to their own lines. Thus they combine the mobility of cavalry with the staying-power of infantry; and by daily training and practice they attain such proficiency that even on a steep incline they are able to control the horses at full gallop and to check and turn them in a moment. They can run along the chariot pole, stand on the yoke and get back into the chariot as quick as lightning.'

In this single vivid passage Caesar sums up the skill, the exuberance and the sheer daring of the people. We must, however, remember that he is talking about the upper class – the aristocrats who could afford horses and chariots, and chariot drivers, and could spend much of their time in practising their fighting skills. The average peasant, whose surplus food production supported the excesses of his masters, would have possessed only a shield of wood or leather and a sling and, if he was rich enough, perhaps even a spear and a sword. It would be totally misleading to give the impression that everyone's time and energy was occupied in fighting and display. For most of the population, much of the time would have been spent engrossed in farming activities of the kind considered earlier. Nevertheless it is possible to trace, in the archaeological record, evidence to suggest the appearance of increasingly aggressive trends in society.

There were scattered over the countryside a number of centres where, from time to time, people would have met together in tribal assemblies. The plateau enclosures are one type but there were also ritual enclosures like one found recently at Danebury in Hampshire defined by a series of massive upright timbers. Elsewhere hill-top settlements or pastoral enclosures would have served as meeting-places. From about 600 BC or a little earlier there was a tendency for many of the centres to become defended by ramparts and ditches, and by about 400 BC the countryside was covered with a rash of these hill-forts. As time went on, however, many of them were abandoned while those that remained were made progressively stronger, sometimes with additional lines of defence but always with more and more massively defended entrances. There seems, then, to have been concentration of effort (and presumably population) on selected centres.

Hill-forts vary considerably in size and complexity but those in southern Britain have many characteristics in common. They comprise an enclosed area averaging 10-20 acres in extent defended by a ditch backed by a rampart, which in the earlier periods was usually faced with vertical timber or stone walling. Our knowledge of hill-fort interiors is still very incomplete but recent work has suggested that many of them were densely built up with rows of houses sometimes arranged along streets. Each would have had one or more shrines where the tribal gods were worshipped and there would have been areas where the artisans and craftsmen practised their various skills. In fact the average southern British hill-fort must have been very much like a small town, and like towns they each served as the centre of a rural territory.

Exactly how society was now organised we cannot say in any detail. Strabo mentions that the Britons were ruled by monarchs and Tacitus talks of how the people were distracted between the rival factions of warring chieftains and goes on to say that because of this the people couldn't unite to face the threat of Roman attack when eventually it came in A D 43. Quite possibly each hill-fort served as the base for a chieftain or demi-king, the strength of the defences reflecting the increasing commonness of inter-tribal fighting.

From the time of Caesar's attack in 55 and 54 B C until the landing of the Roman invasion force in A D 43 southern Britain came into closer and closer contact with the Roman world which was, after all, now only a short sea trip away. The importation of Roman luxury goods increased, bringing in, through ports like Hengistbury in Hampshire and Colchester in Essex, large volumes of wine in pottery jars called amphorae, as well as tableware of fine pottery and silver. Exchange was very much easier after the adoption of a coin-economy which served not only for internal commerce but also for overseas trade. In

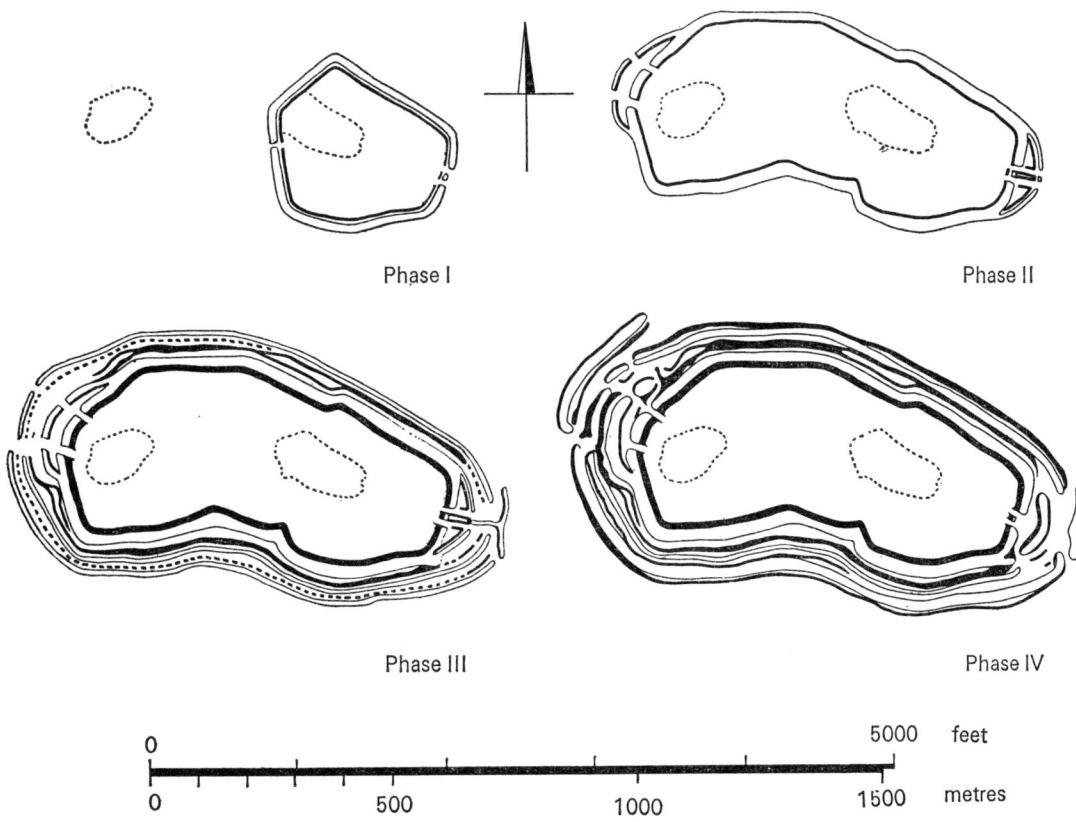

Phase I

Phase II

Phase III

Phase IV

| 0 | | | | 5000 | feet |
| 0 | 500 | 1000 | | 1500 | metres |

Fig 15   Maiden Castle: the development of the Iron Age fort

return for the imports, Britain produced a range of exports listed by Strabo as including corn, cattle, gold, silver, iron, hides, slaves and hunting dogs – all no doubt readily absorbed by the Roman world. The inclusion of slaves in the list is particularly interesting. Before close contact with Rome it is unlikely that the Celts would have bothered much with slaves for themselves, but after the middle of the first century BC the close proximity of the affluent Roman consumer society, based on slavery, provided a new market which the British chieftains were evidently ready to exploit. Once slaves became a profitable commodity slave-raiding, with all its socially destructive overtones, would have increased much as it did in West Africa more recently to satisfy the American market. Thus one more aggressive motivation was added to the pattern of Celtic society.

Bravery and flamboyance epitomised the life-style of the Celtic aristocracy: display and boasting were an essential part of existence. Not unexpectedly there developed an art style and a range of fine craftsmanship to suit the psychological needs of those who could afford it. Gold torcs, elaborate shields and swords and horse and chariot fittings of a most luxurious kind were manufactured widely in southern and eastern Britain by schools of very highly skilled craftsmen working for rich patrons. Good design was not only for the rich, as the beautifully decorated pottery found over most of southern Britain shows. We must also suppose there to have been finely decorated woodwork like the few pieces from Glastonbury and Meare and no doubt gaily coloured fabrics. Energetic and sometimes highly sophisticated patterns, together with bright colours, were a common part of everyday life.

In AD 43 the structure and development of Celtic society in southern Britain was dramatically changed by the successful military invasion initiated by the Emperor Claudius. Four legions, together with supporting auxiliaries, landed in Kent and pushed along the north Kentish trackways to the Medway where they were met by the native hordes led by two chieftains Togodubnus and Caratacus. After a battle raging for two days the native force was shattered and the Roman army was able to move on to cross the Thames and eventually, led briefly by Claudius himself, to destroy the seat of native resistance at Camulodunum (modern Colchester). Thereafter the force split up: the ninth legion moved north into Norfolk and Lincolnshire, the fourteenth spread out through the Midlands, the second was sent against the south and west, and the twentieth was kept in reserve for a while at Camulodunum.

It is the activities of the second legion which particularly concern us here. The legion, the full title of which was the *legio II augusta*, was led by an able young commander, Vespasian, who, 26 years later, was to become Emperor. It seems that the Chichester area was probably controlled at this time by the local client king Tiberius Claudius Cogidubnus, who served both as a native king and a Roman administrator. If so, the protected harbours of the Chichester region would probably have been used as the springboard for Vespasian's advance across the west of Britain. One contemporary historical account tells how he conquered the Isle of Wight, overcame two powerful tribes and destroyed more than twenty fortified native capitals. The implications of this brief account, that the west remained hostile to Rome to the last, are dramatically borne out by the archaeological evidence.

Excavations in several of the hill-forts west of the River Test, many of which must number among the twenty captured by Vespasian, have produced clear traces of defence against Roman attack. At Hod Hill the old settlement was softened up by Roman ballista fire before being taken; at Maiden Castle the defenders, slaughtered by the Romans, were hastily buried in a cemetery at the east gate, while at South Cadbury the remains of the inhabitants, including women and children, were left unburied on one of the roadways. In spite of their massive defences, the native forts were no match for Roman tactics: they were, after all, designed against casual raid rather than the organised siege warfare of the Roman army. Faced with the relentless efficiency of the Roman military machine, native opposition, for all its valour and energy, inevitably crumbled.

In Dorset, some measure of continued local resistance is demonstrated by the dense network of forts which the military authorities felt it necessary to construct and to maintain in good order for at least a decade after the invasion, to keep an eye on the newly conquered territory. New roadways made communications more rapid, supply bases were established on the coasts and somewhere, perhaps beneath Dorchester, lay the headquarters base of the legion with its administrative establishment and reserves of men and equipment, always at the ready if there looked like being trouble in any outlying part. By 47 a frontier zone had been established in advance of the line of the Fosse Way which ran from Lyme Bay through Bath and Cirencester up to Lincoln, but the line was gradually abandoned and by the 60s the army had pulled out of the south leaving it for the administrators to organise into a law-abiding and profitable part of the new province.

Most parts of southern Britain can boast large numbers of hill-forts dating to the period from about 600 BC to AD 43. The best way to appreciate the density of these fortifications is to examine the Ordnance Survey map of Iron Age Britain – an essential document for anyone interested in the period. As the name implies, hill-forts tend to be sited on hill-tops or ridge ends, usually in a prominent and commanding position. Many of them are easily accessible but most are on private land and permission to visit them should be obtained from the owners.

Danebury, *Hampshire* (grid ref. SU 324377)

3 miles north-west of Stockbridge: reached by turning off the A30 half a mile from the town and following the signposts. The site belongs to the Hampshire County Council and is available to visitors at all times.

The earthworks of the hill-fort now lie within a beech wood. The main defences consist of a bank and ditch with a further bank on the outer lip of the ditch, created by dumping the spoil from periodic ditch clearings while the fort was in use. When originally built in the fourth century BC, the rampart was faced

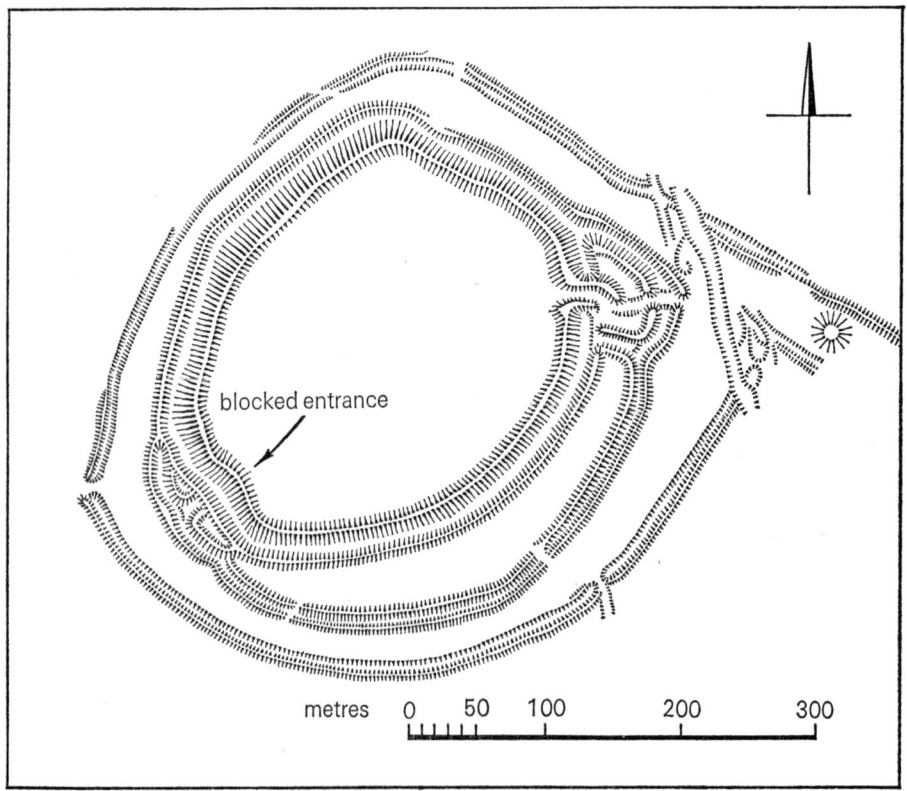

blocked entrance

metres 0 50 100 200 300

Fig 16 Plan of the Iron Age hill-fort at Danebury, Hants

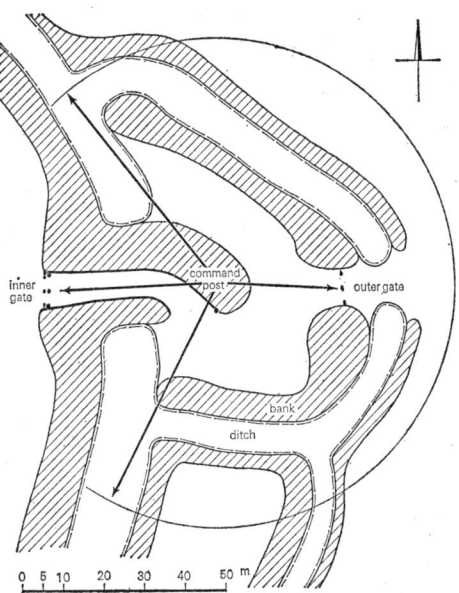

Fig 17 The East entrance at Danebury showing the area in range of slingstones fired from the command post

inner gate

command post

outer gate

bank

ditch

0 5 10   20   30   40   50 m

with vertical timbers. In the third or second century the ditch was recut to a V–shaped profile while at the same time the bank was remodelled to create a steeply sloping outer face capped on the crest with a flint-built wall. Later still, after many years of use followed by a period of disuse, the ditch was again recut and the rampart heightened possibly at the time of the Roman invasion.

The fort was provided with two gates. The south-west gate was blocked up during the time when the fort was in use but its position and outworks can still be traced. The east gate is very well preserved and has been excavated. Originally it was a simple structure but as time went on it became more elaborate until, about 100 BC, a series of major modifications were undertaken resulting in a complex of forward-projecting earthworks together with an outer-gate, designed to protect a long corridor approach, lined with near-vertical flint walling, which lay in front of the main timber-built gateway. One of the curved earthworks served as a command post from which all parts of the entrance could be viewed. From here defenders armed with slings could easily have picked off anyone attempting to approach the entrance. The entire complex had clearly been very carefully planned with its defensive potential firmly in mind.

Attached to the south side of the fort is a crescent-shaped enclosure, defended by a bank and ditch, which probably served as a corral for cattle. Later, a new ditch was dug all round the fort to create another somewhat larger enclosure for livestock. Beyond this ditch, traces of the celtic fields can be seen.

No trace survives on the surface of the buildings inside the fort but recent excavations have shown that the interior was very heavily occupied.

Maiden Castle, *Dorset* (grid ref. SY 667885)

2 miles south-west of Dorchester: reached by leaving Dorchester on the Weymouth road, A354, and turning off right following the signposts. The site is under the guardianship of the Department of the Environment.

Maiden Castle is probably the most impressive hill-fort in southern Britain. It covers more than 45 acres in its most extended form. The earliest occupation on the site is a causewayed camp of 3000-2500 BC, now obliterated by later fortifications. Then followed the construction of a long mound covering a neolithic burial at the east end. The hill-fort began in the fifth century BC as a small enclosure on the eastern knoll of the hill defended by a timber-revetted rampart and a ditch. Later the fortifications were extended to include the western knoll and two entrances with complex outworks were constructed. In the third phase additional lines of earthworks were dug to encircle the hill-top and finally, about 100 BC, further earthworks were added, the existing structures were strengthened and the gates were totally redesigned to include platforms for slingers.

Maiden Castle was attacked and taken by the Romans and its massive gates were dismantled. Some of the native defenders killed at the time were buried in a war cemetery at the east gate.

The internal structures of the pre-Roman period included a number of houses and storage pits, internal roads and probably a shrine which was rebuilt in masonry in the late Roman period.

The finds from the excavations carried out in 1934-8 are displayed in the Dorset County Museum at Dorchester.

Hod Hill, *Dorset* (grid ref. SU 855106)

4 miles north-west of Blanford Forum close to the A350. The fort is privately owned.

Hod Hill is important both for its native hill-fort and for a magnificently preserved Roman fort built in one corner. The pre-Roman fort was a univalate structure (one bank and ditch) until just before the Roman conquest when there is evidence of a hasty attempt at strengthening by adding a line of outer defences. One of the most remarkable features of the site are the exceptionally clear earthworks belonging to densely packed circular houses which once occupied the south-eastern quarter of the enclosure before the Roman invasion. When the vegetation is low it is possible to trace the position of the huts, their storage pits, the pathways between them and some of their enclosing ditches. Over the rest of the interior ploughing has obliterated the surface features.

The north-west corner of the native fort was partitioned off in AD 43 by the much slighter, but scientifically designed, ditches and ramparts put up to protect the Roman garrison which was stationed here for some years after the invasion

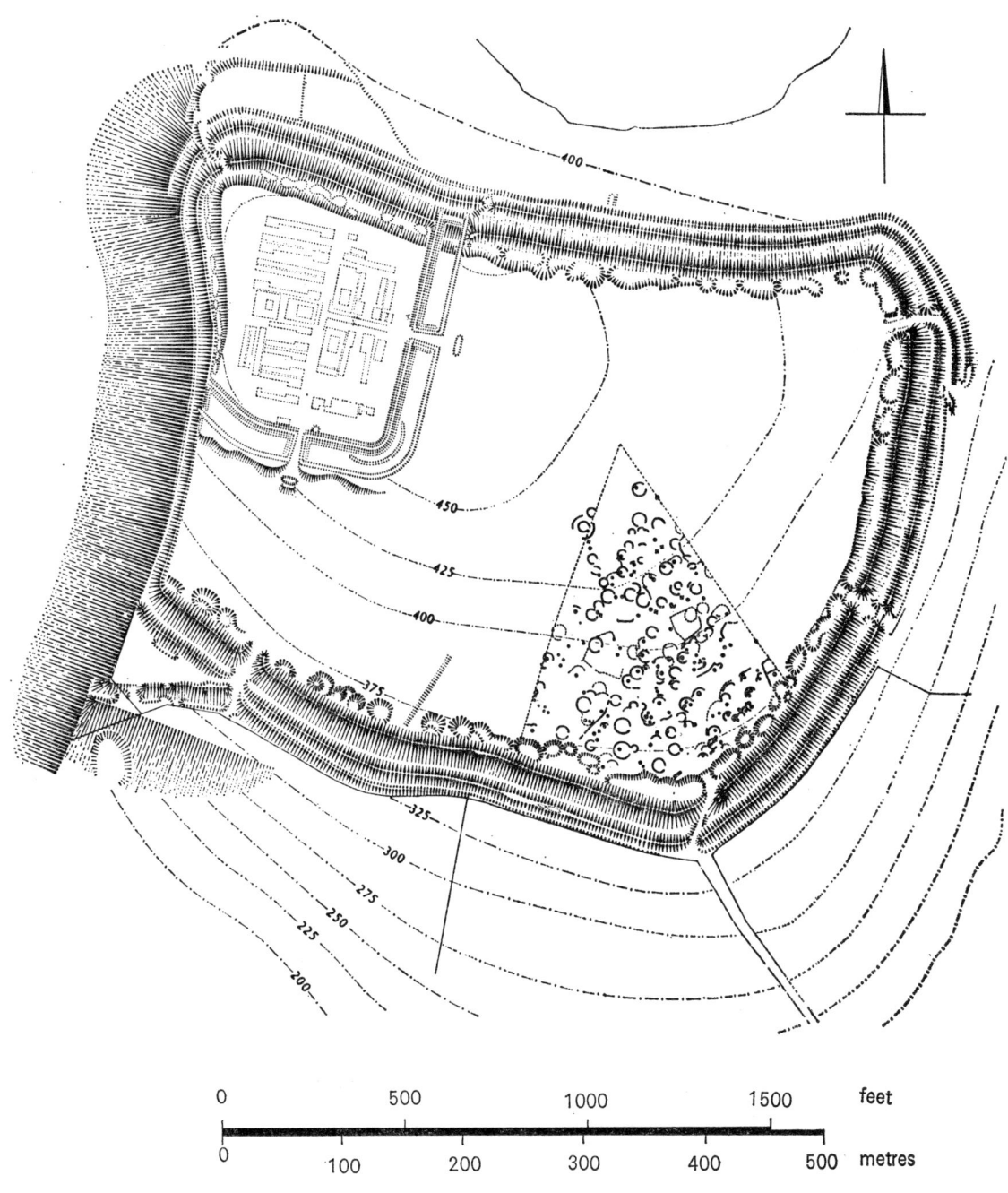

0	500	1000	1500	feet
0	100	200	300	400	500	metres

Fig 18 *Hod Hill, Dorset, showing the Roman fort built in the corner of the Iron Age fort. The triangular area in the south-east corner is unploughed and still contains the well-preserved earthworks of the Iron Age houses. (see also fig 18a overleaf)*

to keep the area under control. The two gates can be traced together with the earthworks protecting them (compare the careful simplicity of these Roman gates with the brute force behind the concept of the earlier Danebury gate). Just inside the gates were earthen platforms to support the ballistae placed so as to be able to hurl missiles at any attacker.

Inside the defences of the Roman fort were a series of timber buildings provid-

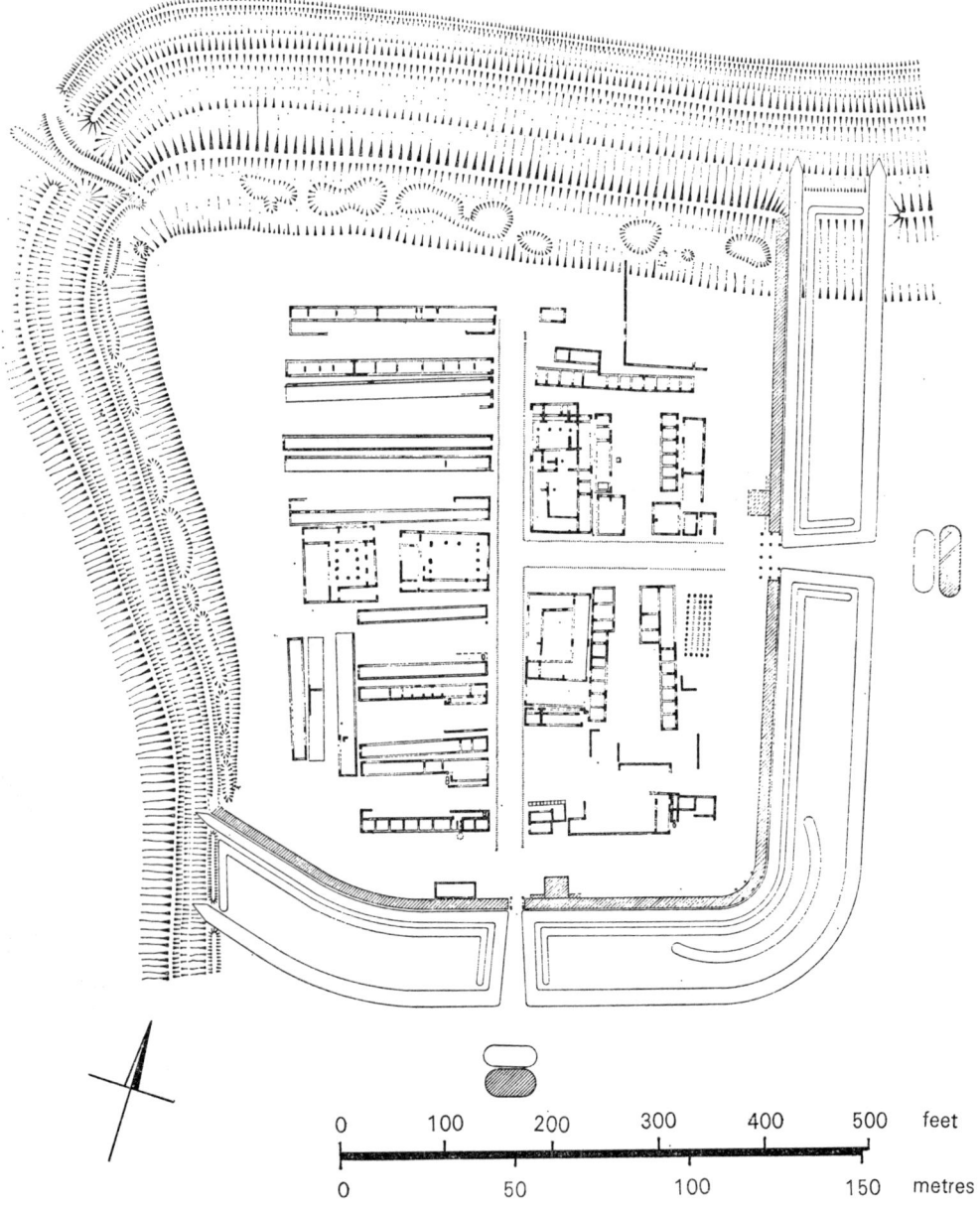

Fig 18a *Detail of the Roman fort at Hod Hill*

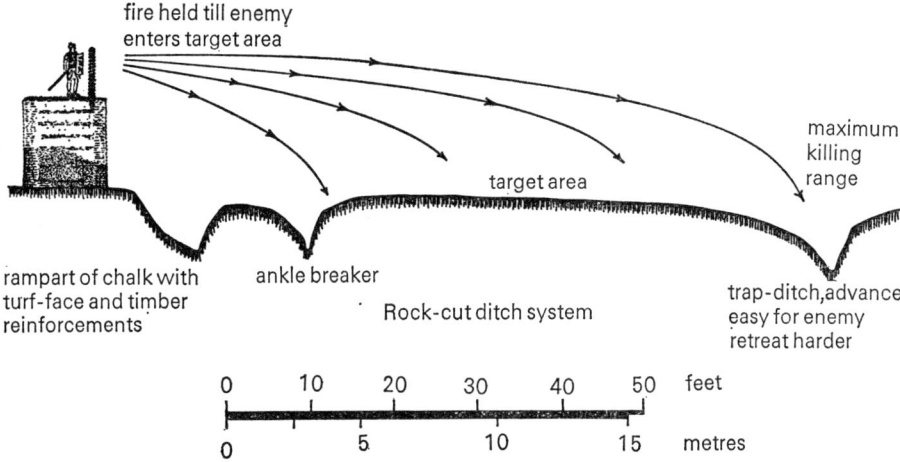

Fig 19 *Hod Hill, the defensive system of the Roman fort*

ing the administrative and living quarters for the troops as well as storage and stabling. The platforms for these structures and the positions of the roadways can still be made out.

All the finds from the excavations are now in the British Museum.

Other hill-forts

There are hundreds of other hill-forts which can be visited but the list is far too long to include here. Most of them preserve characteristics of the kind mentioned in the three examples described above. All the major sites with surviving earthworks are shown on the 1-inch Ordnance Survey maps.

Art and weapons of display

Most provincial museums possess material belonging to the 600 years before the Roman invasion, but much of the aristocratic metalwork of the period has found its way into the collections of the British Museum where the best objects are on permanent display.

5. The Roman Peace

The effect of Rome on the lives of the British people was immediate if not dramatic. In the south, inter-tribal warring was halted, liberating the energies that previously had been dissipated on display and aggression. In its place the imposed system of Roman capitalism offered a new and, to some, an immediately acceptable pattern within which to live. Surplus could be turned into money, money could be accumulated or invested, and amassed wealth could be used to buy status and the trappings of affluence such as country estates or town houses. In short, a good measure of the surplus that had previously been wasted was now ploughed back into the civilised structure of Romano-British life.

The central element behind the commercial prosperity of the new province was an efficient system of government and marketing; both hinged on the development of towns. There were, of course, towns in the pre-Roman period. In many respects the old hill-forts must have served as urban centres, but there were also larger agglomerations, towns like Verulamium and Camulodunum which were later to develop as Roman cities. In their pre-Roman form these were large, straggling collections of timber buildings where trade and industry were practised on a large scale, and the coins of the local dynasties were minted. Similar centres existed at Calleva (Silchester) and probably at Selsey, south of Chichester, Canterbury and Winchester as well as on Hengistbury Head in Hampshire, which unlike the rest failed to develop later as a Roman centre.

The attitude of the new Government was simple but well considered. The country was divided up into a number of administrative units based on the old tribal groups, and an urban centre was established in each, wherever possible taking over from an existing centre either on the same site or close by. Thus Maiden Castle, which had been one of the principal towns of the Durotriges, was soon superseded by Durnovaria (Dorchester), a few miles away, while Noviomagus (Chichester) developed on a new site at the expense of the old tribal oppidum, based somewhere on the Selsey peninsula. Elsewhere, for example at Silchester and Canterbury, the Roman establishments occupied the same sites as their predecessors.

The significance of the town as a civilising and stabilising factor was fully appreciated by the Roman governors. Julius Agricola, governor between AD 78 and 84, is reported by his biographer Tacitus to have forwarded the process of urbanisation with some enthusiasm.

'To induce a people, hitherto scattered, uncivilised and therefore prone to fight, to grow pleasurably inured to peace and ease, Agricola gave private encouragement and official assistance to the building of temples, public squares and private mansions. He praised the keen and scolded the slack, and competition to gain honour from him was as effective as compulsion. Furthermore, he trained the sons of the chiefs in the liberal arts and expressed a preference for British natural ability over the trained skill of the Gauls. The result was that in place of distaste of the Latin language it became a passion to command it. In the same way, our national dress came into favour and the toga was everywhere to be seen. And so the Britons were gradually led on to the amenities that make vice agreeable – arcades, baths and sumptuous banquets. They spoke of such novelties as "civilisation", when really they were only a feature of enslavement.' There can hardly have been a clearer statement of policy.

The reasons why sites were chosen for urban development varied enormously. Some, as we have seen, were already occupied, others developed around military bases, benefiting from the military communication system and the ready market which the soldiers provided, to maintain their hold until the army moved out and development could continue unhindered. Other towns grew up for purely economic reasons like the port at Dover and the great trading centre at London which, by AD 60, was 'teeming with traders and merchants'. Towns were not everywhere successful, some failed, others remained static, but for the most part development was remarkably consistent over most of the country.

Most of the towns began as little more than collections of simple timber buildings lining the few gravelled roads that had been laid out at the time. Then, in the late 70s and 80s, masonry public buildings were erected in some of the more progressive towns. The buildings of the forum and basilica which served as the civic centre were usually the first, together with ancillary structures like public baths and amphitheatres. It was at about this time that some of the towns were provided with their early grid of streets, though in others streets were not properly organised until several decades later. Gradually, more buildings were put up and the towns began to spread. Some centres were surrounded by earthwork defences during the first century but many towns were probably open until the late second century at which time there seems to have been a spate of building town defences. Late second-century defences had certain features in common: they usually consisted of a rampart fronted by a ditch with the main gates built in masonry. Later, in the early years of the third century, the fronts of the ramparts were cut back and a stone wall added butting up to the already existing masonry gate and replacing any timber structures by stone. Why these great acts of civic indulgence were carried out at this time is difficult to say, unless they were to celebrate the gift of citizenship which the Emperor Caracalla bestowed on all the free-born inhabitants of the Empire in AD 212 or 214. By the late third century, the appearance of many of the towns was changing – timber building was giving way to masonry. Indeed, by the early fourth century most

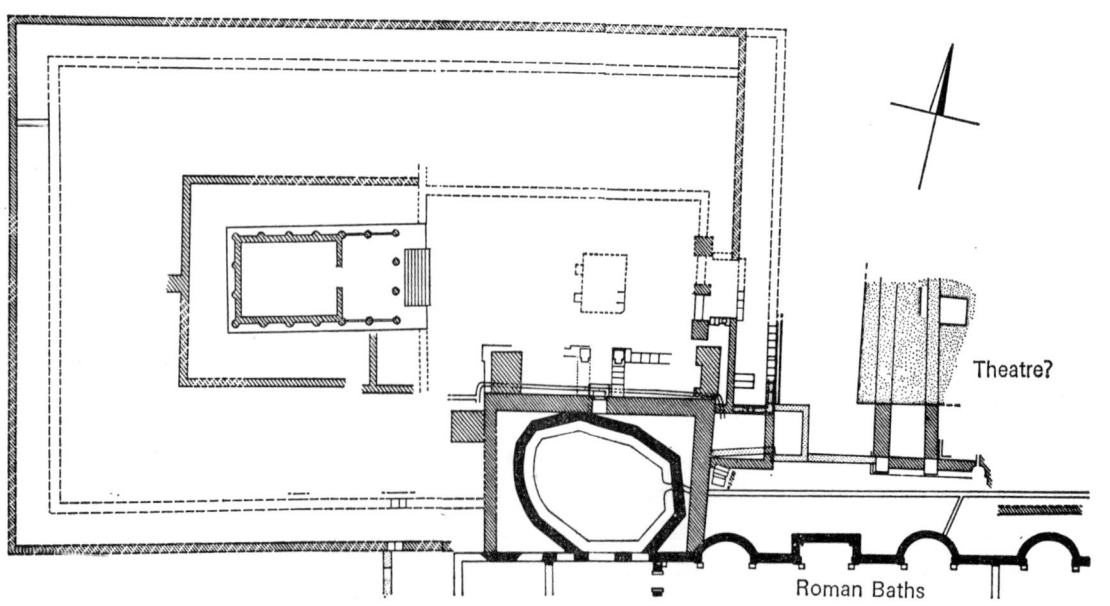

Fig **20** *Reconstruction of the front of the Temple of Sulis Minerva at Bath*

Fig **21** *The Temple of Sulis Minerva at Bath*

Theatre?

Roman Baths

of the buildings, private and public alike, would have been of stone, many of them elaborately decorated with mosaics and painted walls. Thus, in little over 200 years, the style of southern British society had been transformed from heroic warring dissipation to a civilised order comparable with any respectable Roman province on the European mainland, its civic architecture indistinguishable and the pattern of daily life such that a Briton would have felt at home practically anywhere in the Empire.

Roman administrators were adept at conserving those native institutions which they considered to be useful. Social structure was adapted rather than revolutionised. The pattern of regional government was based on a town council, the *ordo*, composed of one hundred local dignitaries called *decurions*, who would become eligible for the office only after acquiring certain property qualifications. In practice the decurions would have been mainly rich natives, many of whose ancestors had been the chieftains and warriors of the pre-Roman era. Local government was in their hands; they would have been responsible for public works, maintenance of roads, organising public entertainment, tax collecting and, to some extent, the dispensation of justice. Representatives from the towns would have met together annually in a National Assembly which was probably modelled to a large extent on the annual gatherings of the preceding periods, the emphasis of the discussions now being the state. The big difference, however, would have been that under Roman government there existed a vast administrative machine over and above the local government, comprised of a governor, a procurator, justices and the complex of civil servants needed to maintain the system.

On the religious level there was probably very little conflict between the old gods and the official gods of the Roman state. In practice it was policy to conflate ancient deities with their nearest Roman counterpart, thus the old native god Lenus was linked to Mars and the composite deity was worshipped as Mars-Lenus. The most dramatic visual reminder of this process is provided by the great religious buildings put up around the sacred spring at Aquae Sulis (Bath). The spring had evidently been presided over by the Celtic deity Sul, who was endowed with certain healing powers. When the time came for the up-grading of the shrine to one of considerable grandeur, it was natural for Sul to be likened to the Roman Minerva and the great temple assigned to the joint goddess Sulis Minerva, whose name appears many times on dedicatory inscriptions. The temple was purely classical in architectural concept, fronted with an impressive carved pediment supported on four Corinthian columns. The central element of the pediment, a great human head, symbolises above all the composite deity. It is the head of a male with all the characteristics of celtic art, a heavy furrowed brow, lentoid eyes, a wedge-shaped nose and a drooping moustache, but its mass of curly hair is mixed up with serpents exactly like the Gorgon's head of classical mythology. The head is shown being carried aloft on a shield by two winged victories in perfect classical stance, while below the shield is an owl perched on a helmet, one of the attributes commonly associated with Minerva. In this single piece of sculpture is symbolised the spirit of religious compromise that formed an essential part of the Roman genius.

Alongside the religious conservatism there were newly introduced concepts. One of these – emperor worship – was far from readily received: its story serves to highlight one aspect of the conflict between Roman and native. At Camulodunum (Colchester) in the centre of the pre-Roman urban complex where the old native war god Camulos must have been worshipped, the Roman administration set up a *colonia* – a planned settlement for veteran soldiers. This process was common enough in newly conquered territories because a colonia was a convenient way of demonstrating the comforts of Roman urban life to the natives while at the same time getting over the problem of what to do with retired soldiers, and providing a nucleus of trained military men in areas which might still prove to be politically unstable. The policy worked well enough in most places, but at Camulodunum there was immediate conflict for a number of reasons, one of which was the setting up of a great temple dedicated to the deified Emperor Claudius. It may be that the thinking behind the move was an attempt to focus British nationalism on the head of the Roman state. At any event the policy was a serious error of judgement, not the least because it would have been considered an enormous slight to the old god Camulos to have had his position usurped in this way. When, in A D 60, a rebellion broke out in Britain led by the famous East Anglian queen Boudicca, one of the targets that the rebels made for was the colonia and the temple, eventually destroying both and slaughtering the veterans who ran to shelter in the building. It is a measure of Roman power that both colonia and temple were rebuilt soon after the rebellion was put down.

One of the most far-reaching effects of Romanisation in Britain was the emergence of a truly cosmopolitan society. At any one time there must have been tens of thousands of foreigners present in the country, all contributing to the gradually evolving culture of the province. Totally new gods were introduced, some of them alien to British traditions such as the Eastern mystery religions involving the worship of deities like Mithras, Isis, Serapis and Christ. Generally an atmosphere of religious tolerance prevailed except for a period in the fourth century when the Christians were actively trying to stamp out other religions, but the persecution passed and in the late fourth century paganism revived.

The army was the principal means by which continentals were introduced into this country. A glance at the army lists, reconstructed from inscriptions and a few texts, demonstrates the presence of Gauls, Spaniards, Moroccans, Germans, Sarmatians and troops whose home lay as far away as Mesopotamia. Along with the troops would have come specialists like the Greek doctor stationed at Chester whose existence is indicated by a recently discovered inscription from the town. Sometimes it is possible to delve a little more deeply into the lives of the immigrants. One man called Barates, who was a standard-maker, came to Britain from Palmyra in Syria and while he was here he married Regina, a Catuvellaunian girl, whose home would have been somewhere in Essex. They spent their life together in the military zone on Hadrian's Wall and eventually died there. This single family history, reconstructed from their tombstones, is probably representative of the processes of immigration and intermarriage which were going on continuously throughout the four centuries of Roman occupation.

Complete freedom of movement, and a governmental system which encouraged the frequent change of senior administrators, meant that the governors of Britain came to this country for their short terms of office after serving in widely separated parts of the Empire. Invariably they brought with them their entourage of supporters and dependants, many of whom would have engaged in trade and commerce while they were here. In the early years of the occupation the developing towns must have looked like the boom towns of America in the last century, bustling with all kinds of commercial and speculative activity. Systems of accounting, literacy, middle-men, quick returns, in fact all the elements of the complex capitalist system are beautifully summed up in the text of a writing tablet found in the River Walbrook in London:

'Rufus, son of Callisunus, greetings to Epillicus and all his fellows. I believe you know I am well. If you have made the list, please send. Do look after everything carefully. See that you turn the slave girl into cash...'

SITES TO VISIT
Roman Towns
Southern Britain was densely scattered with towns of varying sizes: the major examples are shown on the plan (Fig. 25). A rather more complete picture is provided by the Ordnance Survey map of Roman Britain which includes minor settlements, roads and other remains but the map was published in 1956 and is, therefore, out of date.

Most of the principal towns of the south have continued to be occupied on the same site since the Roman period – a fact which has meant that Roman features, where they survive, are usually buried beneath many feet of later accumulations and there is seldom much to see. Two towns, Calleva (Silchester) and Verulamium (near St Albans), were, however, not subsequently built over.

Both have been extensively excavated and the basic outlines of their plans are known. The Silchester excavations were carried out before modern archaeological techniques had developed, thus while the ground plan of the town's masonry buildings is well known, there is little that can be said of the earlier stages of its development when structures were of timber. At Verulamium, on the other hand, the modern excavations were more restricted in extent but the amount of information recovered, particularly about the early phases, was considerable. Together the two sites typify most facets of Roman town life.

It would be impossible here to list everything that remains to be seen of our Roman towns, but the following suggestions cover all the major visible aspects of urban life.

Verulamium, *Hertfordshire*

The Roman town is situated on the north-western outskirts of St Albans. The Verulamium Museum in St Michael's Street, close to St Michael's church, is the best place to begin a visit. Finds from the excavations are extensively displayed together with explanatory material giving information about parts of the Roman town which can still be seen. The museum contains the finest collection of Roman mosaics and wall paintings in the country, outside the British Museum.

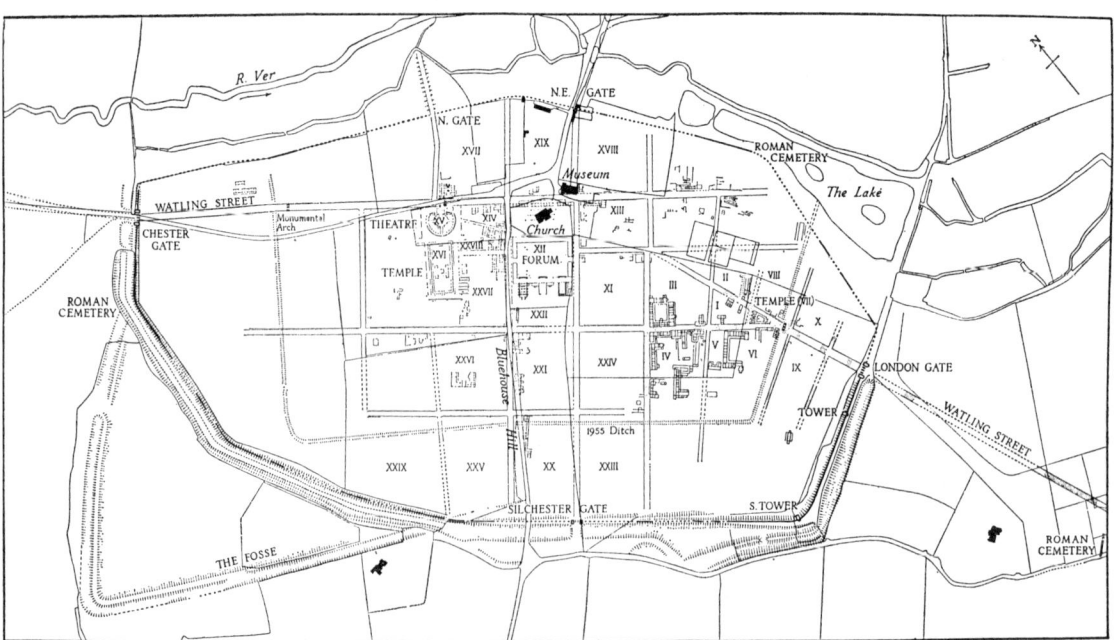

Fig 22 The Roman city of Verulamium

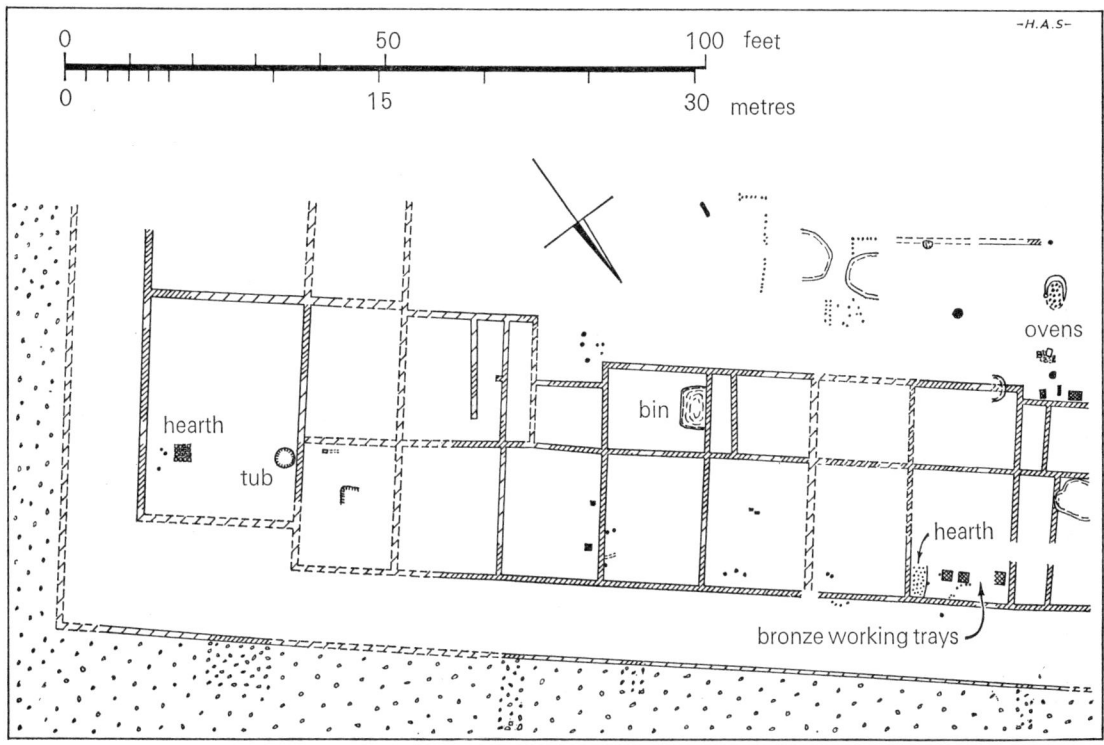

Fig 23 Verulamium: Roman timber built shops destroyed in AD 60

The city wall survives along much of the south side of the town with its ramparts, internal turrets and bastions. The foundations of the great south gate by which the main road from London entered are also exposed.

The theatre, which lay towards the centre of the city, is fully displayed, together with a ground plan of early timber-built shops and the foundations of a substantial masonry town house complete with an underground shrine. Another town house with elaborate mosaic pavement and a hypocaust beneath it is open to inspection in the park not far from the museum.

Dorchester, *Dorset*
The line of the Roman and medieval city walls is marked by the 'Walks' – tree lined paths laid out in the eighteenth century, but only one piece of Roman masonry survives, in West Walks just south of the West gate which stood near the 'Top of Town'.

The well-preserved foundations of a town house are exposed behind the County Council offices in Colliton Park.

The amphitheatre known as Malmsbury Rings is just south of the town on the road to Weymouth.

Finds from the town are in the Dorset County Museum, in Dorchester.

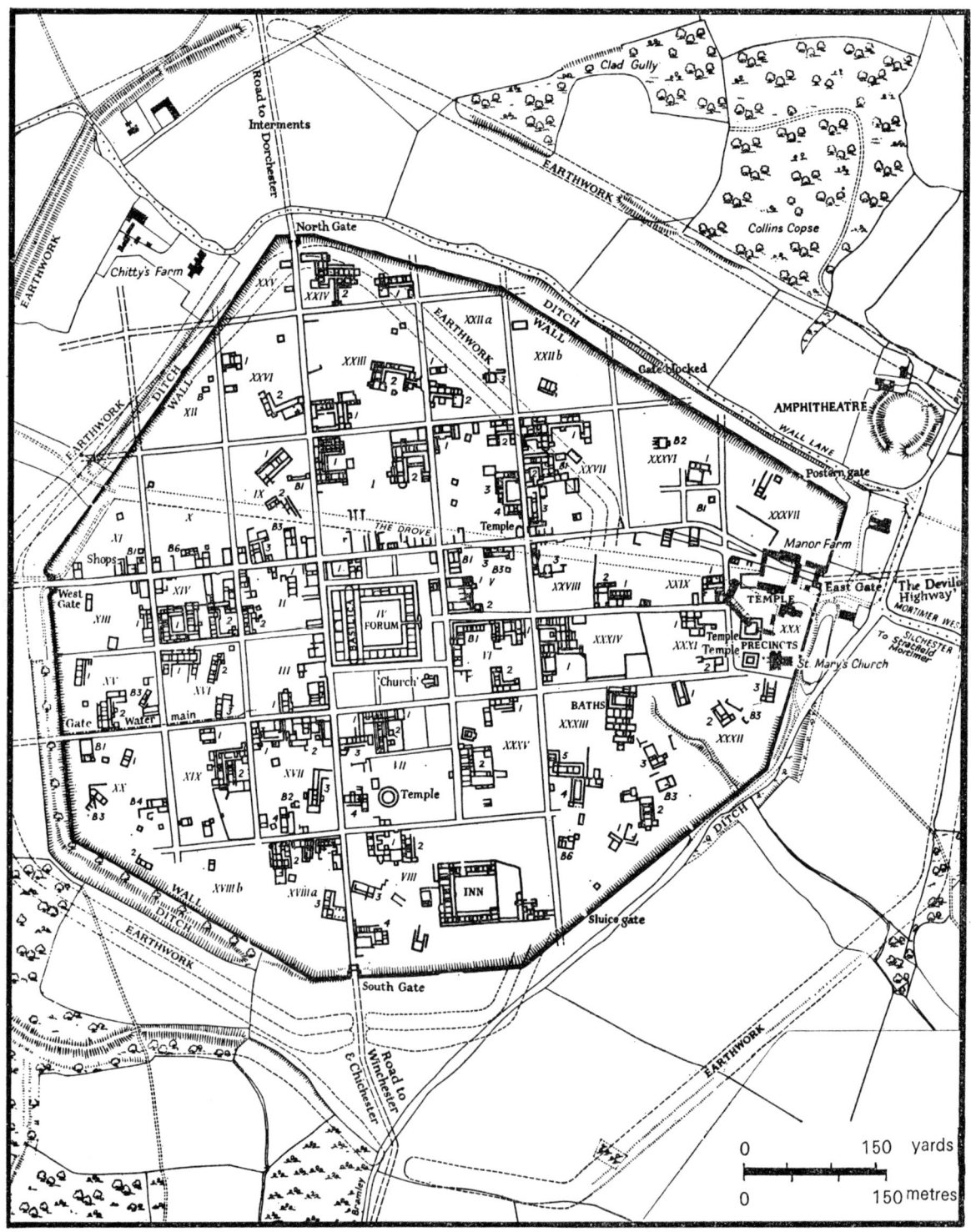

Fig 23 *Plan of Roman Silchester*

Silchester, *Hampshire*

Silchester is far less visual. The city walls still survive around the entire circuit of the town, but they enclose now only fields, the old excavation having been entirely refilled. Just outside the north-east corner of the town the overgrown earthworks of the amphitheatre can be traced.

Most of the material from the excavation is in the Reading Museum.

Bath, *Somerset*

Bath was a minor centre in the Roman period, only 23 acres compared with the average town of 100 or more acres, but it was adorned with some of the most impressive architecture in the province, put up around its sacred spring. There were two principal buildings, a great temple dedicated to Sulis Minerva and a

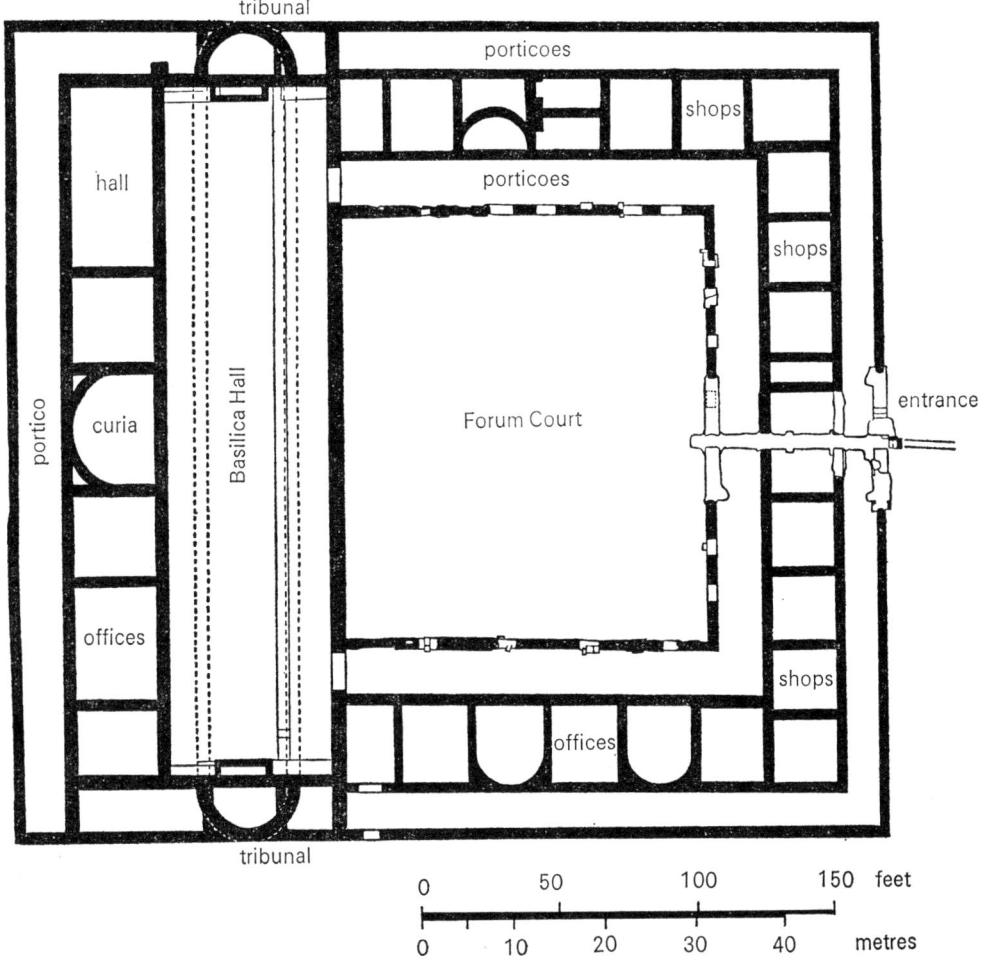

Fig 24 The Forum and Basilica at Silchester

bathing establishment immediately adjacent to it. The temple lies now beneath the Pump Room, Stall Street and the Abbey yard and there is little of the actual foundation to be seen but a considerable quantity of the architectural detail belonging to the superstructure is on display in the Roman Baths Museum, including the famous Gorgon's head pediment. The Roman Baths themselves are extensively displayed and must constitute one of the most dramatic Roman buildings to be seen in Britain. More of the establishment, excavated in the 1880s, is at present hidden from view in nearby cellars.

The Roman Baths Museum houses a very comprehensive collection of Roman sculpture from the town and from its cemeteries.

Winchester, *Hampshire*

Winchester was one of the largest of the Roman towns of southern Britain, but little now survives above ground apart from the city wall in the north-west corner (obscured) and the south-east corner where it has been largely refaced in medieval and later times.

Finds from the town are displayed in the Winchester City Museum.

Chichester, *Sussex*

Chichester still retains much of its city wall which is basically Roman though considerably refaced. Along the south-east and south sides the wall and ditches are particularly well preserved together with remains of the forward-projecting bastions which were added in the late fourth century.

The only notable Roman feature within the walls is an inscription carved on Purbeck marble, which mentions the local king Tiberius Claudius Cogidubnus. It is now exhibited in the wall of the Assembly Rooms in North Street close to the site where it was found.

Outside the town wall to the south-east the earthworks of the amphitheatre can still be traced.

Finds from the city are preserved in the City Museum.

Other Towns

The above brief notes have been restricted to the towns of the south (except for Verulamium) but many others in south-eastern Britain, outside the range of this book, possess visible structures and fine museum collections. Among these should be noted Canterbury, London, Colchester, Cirencester and Gloucester; and even farther afield we might add Leicester, Lincoln, York, Wroxeter (near Shrewsbury), Caerwent and Chester. All are worthy of a visit.

6. Order into Chaos

During the first two centuries of peace which followed the Roman conquest the economy of the country flourished. With the growth of the towns, providing a stable market for the sale of farm produce, local farmers and smallholders could be assured of a regular income so long as the fertility of the land and the health of their livestock was maintained. Those who, by virtue of the richness of the soil, could produce a large surplus were able to accumulate cash which could be used to purchase a wide range of consumer goods from the market, or could be hoarded and reinvested in more land, stock, or other installations.

The careful excavation of Roman villa sites often allows this process of increasing affluence to be traced in terms of actual structures. Bignor near Pulborough in Sussex provides an excellent example of the development of a villa estate. The site had been occupied from as early as the late first century but the early house has not yet been discovered. As late as the beginning of the third century the owner could only afford a modest but comfortable timber-built farm-house. Sometime after A D 225 the house was rebuilt in stone but even then it was still a simple structure of four rooms only later to be fronted by a corridor. Next, minor additions were made at either end probably more to improve the visual appearance than to increase the floor space. Major extensions came in the fourth century when the existing house was greatly increased in size by being incorporated as one side of a complex of four wings enclosing a courtyard. At this stage a suite of baths was added. The greatest elaboration was reached only in the final stage with the further extension of the north wing to include a suite of rooms for summer use provided with a fountain, and a winter range with central heating. It was at this time, to complete the luxury, that a series of magnificent mosaic floors were laid.

While the interest of Bignor understandably focuses on the elaborate fittings of the house it should be remembered that the house itself formed only a part of the villa establishment. To the east lay a large walled farmyard provided with barns and store buildings while to the south were further buildings which might have been the servants' quarters. The villa was essentially the centre of an estate and as such had to provide not only a comfortable residence for the owner and sufficient accommodation for the villa servants, but also storage space, facilities for maintaining the farm equipment and the complex administrative machinery necessary for running the establishment. It was, in fact, a largely self-contained unit.

Bignor, with its exceptional richness, was not typical of Roman villas as a whole. Only about ten per cent of those at present known could boast patterned

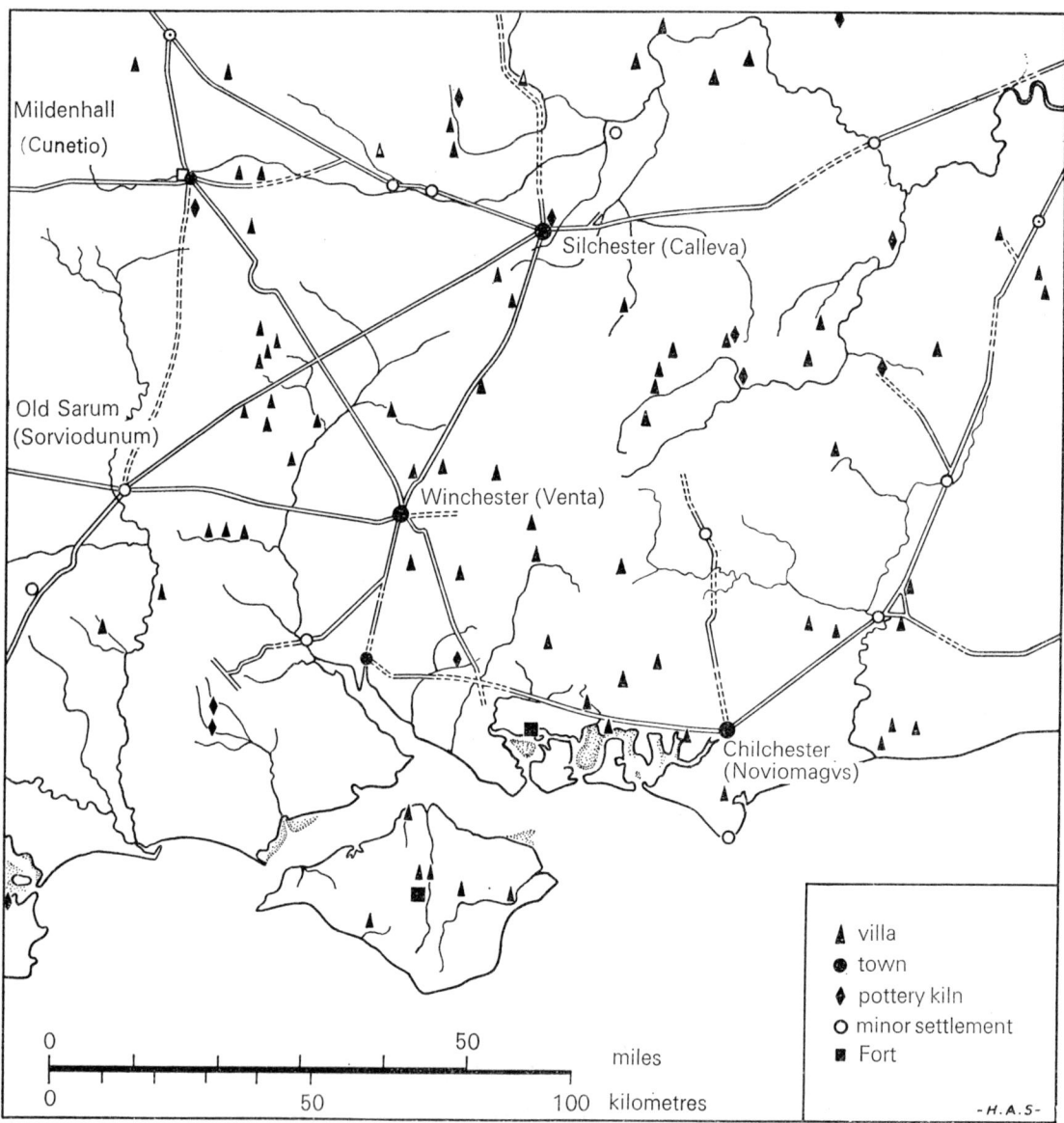

Fig 25 Central southern Britain in the Roman period

mosaics. Most of them were little more than comfortable farm-houses of which a few might have been owned by those wealthy enough to pay for a red tessellated floor, a small heated room or perhaps a bath suite tacked on the end of the house or inserted into an old outbuilding.

Not all of the villas we know of were owner-occupied. Some may have been farms belonging to large estates, run by tenants or bailiffs. Others may have started life as the home farms of privately owned land, later to be bought up by a neighbouring landowner and amalgamated into a larger estate, in which case the villa may have been totally abandoned or it may have been kept on in use as storage space or accommodation for slaves. Both eventualities would be recognisable by means of careful excavation.

While it is true that the villas were largely self-contained, their livelihood depended on easy access to markets. It is hardly surprising, therefore, that most of the villas in the south clustered around the towns usually within a 15 to 20-mile radius, a distance which could have been covered easily in a day by a cart taking produce to market. Another implication of such a settlement pattern is that many of the landowners were sufficiently close to the towns to have served on the town council and may indeed have possessed town houses as well. The close relationship between town and country life is worth emphasising because in an essentially rural province like Britain the dichotomy between urban and rural life would have been far less noticeable than it is today.

With the growth of the large villa estates in the late third century and later, and the increasing desire for the outward and visible signs of affluence which owners would have felt, a climate was created within which artists and craftsmen flourished. A careful study of mosaic pavements has recently shown that a number of schools of mosaicists existed all over the country, probably based on the towns. There seems to have been one such group in Dorchester who worked for the neighbouring villa owners, as well as some of the owners of town houses, going from building to building and laying new floors to the requirements of their patrons. We must suppose that they took with them pattern books, depicting elements of geometric and floral borders and scenes from classical mythology, so that the owners could choose the designs they preferred from the repertoire of the particular school. Most of the floors would have been laid on the spot, the design having been marked out on the damp mortar, by a crafts-man working systematically across the room: one of them actually signed his work in Bignor with the letters TER standing for his name Tertius. If a parti-cularly elaborate picture was required, the mosaicist probably made it up in his workshop, sticking the stones to a sheet of canvas, and then he transported it to the house to be set in position so that the rest of the design could be built up around it.

Mosaics are the most obvious of the craft activities which would have been encouraged by the rich but there were many others which survive less well in the archaeological record. Wall painting was commonly practised, frequently by artists of considerable technical skill, while stucco working and marble veneer-ing, though rarer, played an essential part in interior design. Many of the mov-able fittings for the house were often very elaborate, things like furniture with carved stone legs and stone inlaid tops, and tableware of pewter and silver; all would have been manufactured in workshops in the towns, either as a speculative venture or to the requirements of a particular patron.

The increased affluence of the late Roman period, then, provided an atmosphere in which skilled craftsmen could flourish in much the same way, as the demands of the pre-Roman chieftains for display articles produced the masterpieces of Celtic art. Like the late pre-Roman period the desire for consumer goods spread across the whole social spectrum. There appeared great commercial concerns geared entirely to the manufacture of a single commodity like pottery, salt or shale trinkets. One centre for the manufacture of pottery developed in the New Forest where dozens of kilns and hundreds of tons of potsherds have been found. It seems that the potters got under way on a large scale late in the third century and continued to manufacture much the same range of vessels for more than a hundred years. Basically they aimed at two markets – a local market for coarse wares and a much wider distribution for the finer wares like the glossy purple-coloured beakers that are found over the whole of Britain south of the Thames. Cartloads of their wares would have been sent to the markets in Winchester and Dorchester where the local farmers would have bought them. The pottery was so cheap that even the peasants living in little timber huts in the depths of the countryside could afford to own a few vessels. The dinner tables of fourth-century southern Britain must have presented an appearance of dreary similarity.

For almost two centuries Roman law and order imposed upon the south a peace of a kind which the country had probably never before experienced, but during the third century external troubles began to make an appearance in the form of pirates from the European mainland north of the Rhine. The first response of the British government was to build forts at Brancaster in Norfolk and Reculver in Kent to protect the Wash and the Thames estuary, but as the troubles increased so the coastal fortifications became more numerous. To begin with it seems that the pirates were active only in the North Sea but late in the third century they broke through the English Channel and began to pillage the southern coasts of Britain and the adjacent French shore. In the 280s a Belgian sailor, Carausius, was appointed to 'rid the seas of Belgica and Armorica of pirates'. First he improved existing installations and then built a series of new forts along the unprotected coasts, but soon a quarrel broke out and he was eventually forced to flee the continent and set up an empire of his own in Britain where he remained until he was murdered by one of his lieutenants in 293. One of the reasons put forward for his disenchantment with the central government was that they had accused him of being in league with the pirates, letting them land and plunder the coast, and then meeting them at sea to share the booty. Whatever the truth is in the accusation it gives an interesting insight into the kind of problems facing the province at the time.

The forts put up in the late third century symbolised the change in attitude now coming about – they were essentially defensive structures with massive stone walls, carefully defended gates, and forward-projecting bastions built so as to provide a fighting platform from which the occupants could beat off an attack. Rome was at last on the run.

The history of the last hundred years of Roman occupation is one of gradual breakdown in economy, government and morale, each destructive factor enhancing the effect of the others. External threats became increasingly more serious not only from the Germanic Continent but also from the Picts in Scotland and the Scots in Ireland. The year 367 saw a devastating raid by a band of barbarians who caused chaos as far south as the Thames, the effects of which were only mopped up with some difficulty two years later.

All this time the political power of the army was becoming stronger and commanders were now sometimes directed by the will of their own men. There were growing pressures on the leaders of the British frontier troops to take the army abroad to fight the barbarians, officially in the belief that this was the best way to protect Britain, but in practice the glories and rewards of an expedition to Europe were more attractive than spending a lifetime patrolling Hadrian's Wall. Three times, between 388 and 409, massive armies raised in Britain left to fight in Europe – few of them are likely to have returned. Another factor which was beginning to reach serious proportions was depopulation. Most of the Roman world was, by this time, suffering from a gradual decline in birth rate. Large tracts of countryside were left abandoned and recruitment for the army was made more difficult. To counter these trends barbarians from north of the Rhine-Danube frontier were encouraged to settle in depopulated areas or to fight as mercenaries in the Roman army. While it is not known just how serious population decline was in Britain, it seems most unlikely that the province was an exception to the rule. Indeed it is now evident that large numbers of Germanic mercenaries were serving here by the end of the fourth century. The embarkation of three major armies in a period of just over 20 years would have had a dramatic effect on the population, creaming off a high percentage of the available manpower.

To add to the problems, law and order began to break down. Many parts of the country would have been infested with gangs of bandits made up of deserters from the army, scattered groups of foreign raiders and natives who, for economic reasons, had become drop-outs. In this atmosphere of growing insecurity the towns became more important as defended enclaves. Their defences were improved by the addition of forward-projecting bastions to the walls and most of them were by now guarded by a militia composed in part of Germanic mercenaries. In 409, after the departure of the last major fighting force, the situation became serious; indeed it is probable that a rebellion broke out to overthrow the remnants of the Roman administration. At any event the towns remained intact, but in fear they sent a letter to the Emperor Honorius asking for help. The reply, which came in 410, simply refused and told them that they must now look after their own defence. In the total collapse of the economic system which followed, the whole structure of unified government and the money economy broke down. Life continued in the towns and on the large self-contained villa estates for many decades but gradually the trappings of Roman civilisation became diluted until they were finally submerged beneath the increasing wave of immigrants and invaders from the Germanic areas of the continent.

Thus in less than 5,000 years Britain had experienced a major cycle of social development from scattered hunter-gatherer groups to the tattered remains of civilisation. In this period the roots were established from which the next phase of major advance could spring. It required more people from varied origins to create the English nation, but it may fairly be said that the developments we have considered in southern Britain laid the essential basis which gave the later growth its distinctive character.

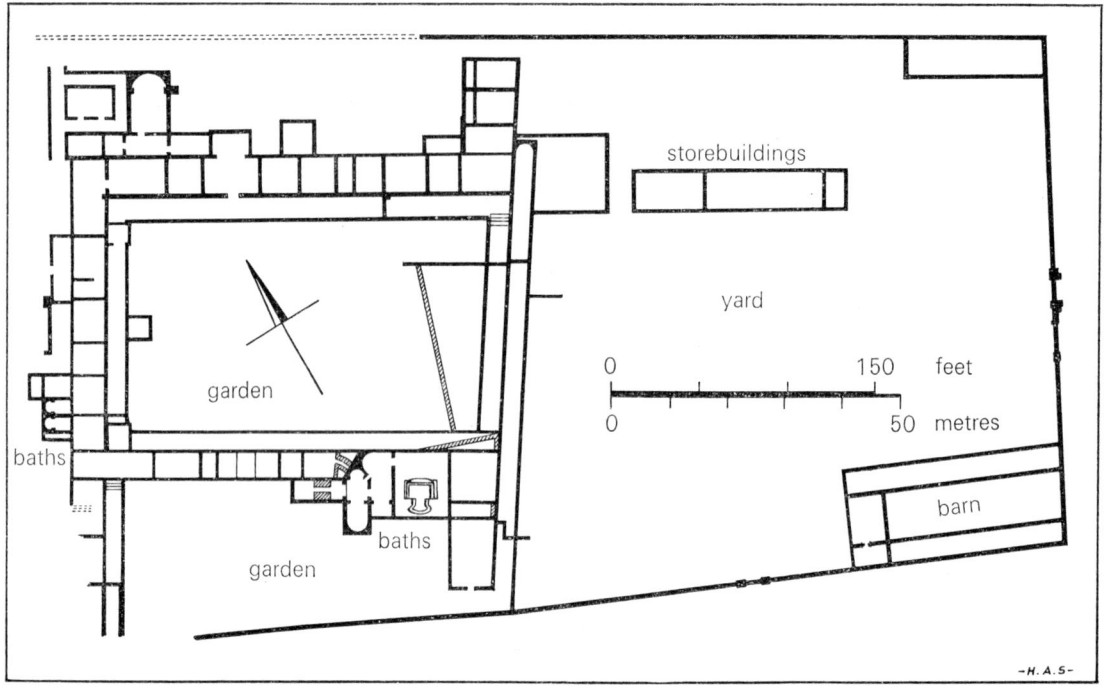

Fig 26 *Plan of the Roman Villa of Bignor Sussex based on the original early 19th Century survey. Fig 27 shows the details at the west wing resulting from modern excavations and a new survey: there are some inconsistences.*

Fig 27   The Roman Villa at Bignor. Three stages in the development of the West Wing

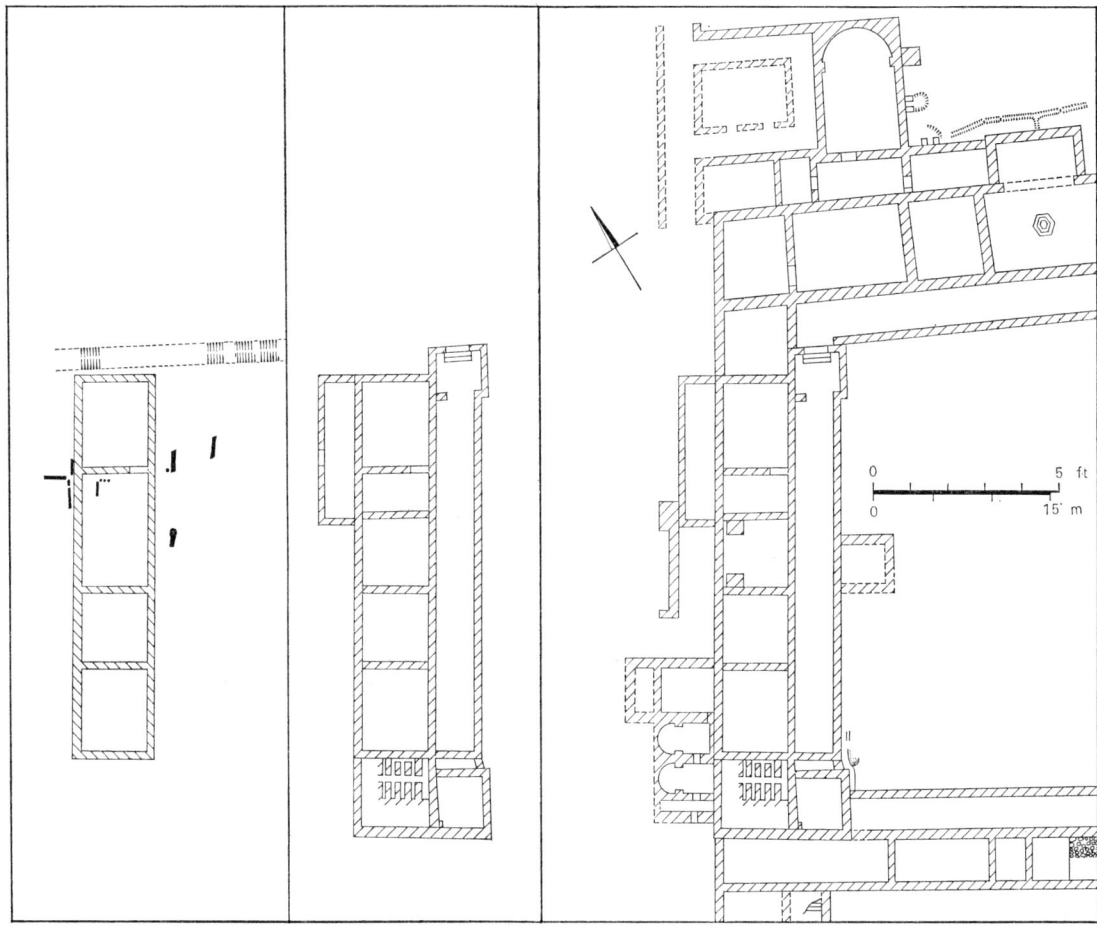

SITES TO VISIT

Roman Villas

Of the many hundreds of Roman villas known in the country only a very few are open to public inspection. The following can, however, be visited:

Bignor, *Sussex* (grid ref. SU988147)

The villa lies midway between the A29 and A285 some ten miles north-east of Chichester, on a shelf of fertile greensand which runs along the edge of the South Downs scarp. Parts of the north wing of the villa are now exposed beneath cover buildings. All the best mosaics, some of them very fine indeed, are on display. The west wing, which formed the nucleus of the original house, is laid out with different coloured asphalt to demonstrate the structural development of the range. Part of the baths and an adjacent mosaic are displayed in the south-east corner of the site.

The finds from the villa are on show in a small site museum.

Fishbourne, *Sussex* (grid ref. SU 838048)

Entrance to the Fishbourne Roman building is obtained by turning off the A259 one and a half miles west of Chichester and following the signposts.

Fishbourne had a long and complex history beginning with simple timber buildings and culminating in the erection of a vast palatial structure in about A D 75-80 which may have been the residence of the local client king Tiberius Claudius Cogidubnus. In this early stage it is totally atypical of the normal Romano-British villa development, but from the early second century the site develops in a more conventional manner until it was destroyed by fire in the 280s.

The entire north wing of the palace, together with all its later developments, is protected by a cover building. In front of it half of the large Roman garden

Fig 28 The Roman villa at Brading, Isle of Wight, based on the original plan of the excavations

has been recreated by selective planting while along the east side the foundations of the east wing have been marked out in the grass.

A site museum displays all the material discovered during the excavation.

Brading, *Isle of Wight* (grid ref. s z 599863)
The villa lies half a mile west of the A3055 south of the village of Brading. The main range of rooms, with several fine mosaics, is protected by a cover building which also houses the collection of finds from the excavation. Various details of the north and south wings can be seen including the baths which were inserted into an out-building on the north side of the courtyard.

Rockbourne, *Hampshire* (grid ref. s u 121171)
The villa lies at the side of the road leading from Sandleheath (2 miles west of Fordingbridge) to Rockbourne. Much of the foundations are now exposed and a site museum houses the collection of finds.

Lullingstone, *Kent* (grid ref. t q 530651)
The site is reached from the village of Eynsford on the A225 between Dartford and Sevenoaks.

The villa, dating from the late first century and continuing in use throughout the Roman period, is extremely well preserved and displayed. It consists of a block of rooms built on several levels with outlying structures including a

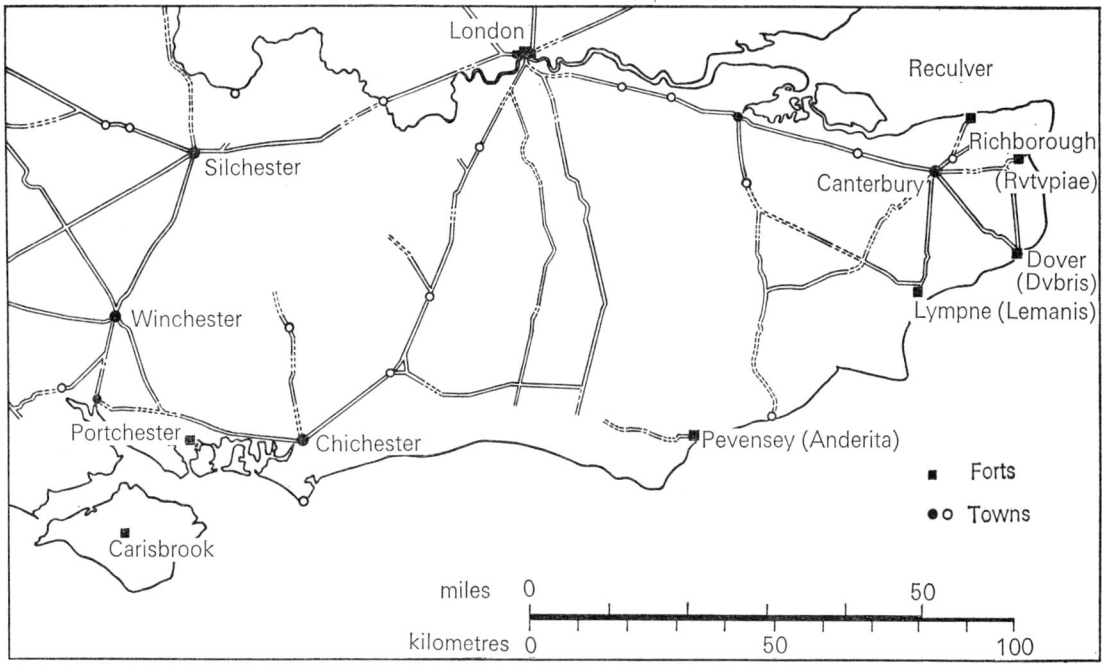

Fig 29   The late Roman shore defences

temple-mausoleum. Some of the rooms were floored with figured mosaic pavements and the walls were elaborately painted. Late in the life of the villa, part of the establishment was turned into a Christian shrine. Most of the finds are displayed on the site but some of the Christian wall paintings and two marble portrait busts are now in the British Museum.

Chedworth, *Gloucestershire* (grid ref. SP053135)

The villa at Chedworth, 8 miles north of Cirencester, lies at the head of a wooded valley. Much of the structure is now preserved and protected including details of bath suites, hypocausts and servants' quarters. The siting and method of display gives an excellent idea of what the villa would have looked like in the Roman period.

The finds are displayed in a site museum.

The late shore defences

The forts erected during the third and fourth centuries around the coasts are shown on the map. All except Dover survive as visible remains and can be visited: Portchester, Pevensey, Richborough and Reculver are Ancient Monuments under the guardianship of the Department of the Environment and are displayed for visitors. Lympne is on private property. The only site museum collection is at Richborough.

Portchester Castle, *Hampshire* (grid ref. SU625045) is the best preserved of the late third-century forts. Its walls, 10 ft thick and 20 ft high, enclose nine acres. The walls were provided with regularly spaced D-shaped bastions to serve as fighting platforms. There were four gates in the centres of each side but only the foundations of part of the west gate can now be seen. The rest are obscured.

Pevensey, *Sussex* (grid ref. TQ645048) was built in the middle of the fourth century. Its plan is more advanced than that of Portchester in that the walls follow the contour of the oval-shaped hill upon which it is built, and the massive bastions are not placed regularly but are spaced so as to command all parts of the wall face.